VAJRADHATU

GARUDA IV

Edited by Chögyam Trungpa, Rinpoche

associate editor Michael H. Kohn

Vajradhatu is an association of Buddhist centers working under the guidance of Chögyam Trungpa, Rinpoche. It publishes Garuda *periodically with the intent of presenting the Buddhist teachings in relation to the spiritual needs of the Western Hemisphere.*

Garuda is published by

VAJRADHATU
1111 Pearl Street
Boulder CO 80302

in association with

SHAMBHALA PUBLICATIONS, INC.
2045 Francisco Street
Berkeley, California
and
68 Carter Lane
London EC4V 5EL

Printed in the United States of America. Distributed in the United States by Random House and in Canada by Random House of Canada, Ltd. Distributed in the Commonwealth by Routledge & Kegan Paul Ltd., London and Henley-on-Thames.

SHAMBHALA
BERKELEY & LONDON

CONTENTS

SUPPLICATION TO THE GURUS OF THE KAGYU LINEAGE

Great Vajradhara, Telo, Naro & Marpa, Mila, the lord of the dharma
Gampopa; the knower of the three times, the omniscient Karmapa; the holders
of the lineage of the four great & the eight lesser schools; Dri, Tak, Tsel,
these three, Sri Drugpa & so on; & those who have completely achieved
the profound path of mahamudra; to those incomparable protectors of all beings
the Dagpo Kagyu – I supplicate you, the Kagyu gurus, I follow your tradition
& example; please grant your blessing.

Renunciation is the foot of meditation, as is said; not being possessed by food
& wealth. To the meditator who cuts off the ties to such a life, grant your blessing, so that he ceases to be attached to honor & ownership.

Devotion is the head of meditation, as is said. It is the guru who opens the
gate to the mine of the profound oral teachings. To the meditator who always
supplicates the guru, grant your blessing, so that true devotion is born in him.

Awareness is the body of meditation, as is said. Whatever thought arises, its nature is nowness. To the meditator who rests there without effort, grant your
blessing, so that the subject of meditation is free from conceptions.

The nature of thoughts is dharmakaya, as is said. Nothing whatever, but everything
arises from it. To the meditator who sees the unobstructed play of the mind, grant
your blessing, so that he realizes the identity of nirvana & samsara.

Through all of my births, may I not be separated from the perfect guru & so
enjoy the glorious dharma. Accomplishing the good qualities of the paths &
the stages, may I speedily attain the state of Vajradhara.

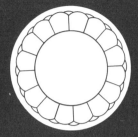

SATIPATTHANA-SUTTA

Thus have I heard. At one time the Blessed One was living among the Kurus, at Kamma-sadamma, a market town of the Kuru people. There the Blessed One addressed the bhikkus thus "Monks," and they replied to him, "Venerable Sir." The Blessed One spoke as follows:

This is the only way, monks, for the purification of beings, for the overcoming of sorrow and lamentation, for the destruction of suffering and grief, for reaching the right path, for the attainment of Nibbana, namely the four Foundations of Mindfulness. What are the four?

Herein a monk lives contemplating the body in the body, ardent, clearly comprehending and mindful, having overcome, in this world, covetousness and grief; he lives contemplating feeling in feelings, ardent, clearly comprehending and mindful, having overcome in this world, covetousness and grief; he lives contemplating consciousness in consciousness, ardent, clearly comprehending and mindful, having overcome, in this world, covetousness and grief; he lives contemplating mental objects in mental objects, ardent, clearly comprehending and mindful, having overcome, in this world, covetousness and grief.

I THE CONTEMPLATION OF THE BODY

And how does a monk live contemplating the body in the body?

Herein, monks, a monk having gone to the forest, to the foot of a tree or to an empty place, sits down, with his legs crossed, keeps his body erect and his mindfulness alert.

Ever mindful he breathes in, and mindful he breathes out. Breathing in a long breath, he knows "I am breathing in a long breath"; breathing out a long breath, he knows "I am breathing out a long breath"; breathing in a short breath, he knows, "I am breathing in a short breath"; breathing out a short breath, he knows "I am breathing out a short breath."

"Experiencing the whole (breath-) body, I shall breathe in," thus he trains himself. "Experiencing the whole (breath-) body, I shall breathe out," thus he trains himself. "Calming the activity of the (breath-) body, I shall breathe in," thus he trains himself. "Calming the activity of the (breath-) body, I shall breathe out," thus he trains himself.

Thus he lives contemplating the body in the body internally, or he lives contemplating the body in the body externally, or he lives contemplating the body in the body, internally and externally. He lives contemplating origination-factors in the body, or he lives contemplating dissolution-factors in the body, or he lives contemplating origination-and-dissolution factors in the body. Or his mindfulness is established with the thought: "The body exists," to the extent necessary just for knowledge and mindfulness, and he lives detached, and clings to naught in the world. Thus also, monks, a monk lives contemplating the body in the body.

And further, monks, a monk knows when he is going "I am going"; he knows when he is standing "I am standing"; he knows when he is sitting "I am sitting"; he knows when he is lying down "I am lying down"; or just as his body is disposed so he knows it.

Thus he lives contemplating the body in the body. . . .

And further, monks, a monk, in going forward and back, applies clear comprehension; in looking straight on and looking away, he applies clear comprehension; in bending and in stretching, he applies clear comprehension; in wearing robes and carrying the bowl, he applies clear comprehension; in eating, drinking, chewing and savoring, he applies clear comprehension; in attending to the calls of nature, he applies clear comprehension; in walking, in standing, in sitting, in falling asleep, in waking, in speaking and in keeping silence, he applies clear comprehension.

Thus he lives contemplating the body in the body. . . .

And further, monks, a monk reflects on this very body enveloped by the skin and full of manifold impurity, from the sole up, and from the top of the head-hair down, thinking thus: "There are in this body hair of the head, hair of the body, nails, teeth, skin, flesh, sinews, bones, marrow, kidney, heart, liver, midriff, spleen, lungs, intestines, mesentery, gorge, faeces, bile, phlegm, pus, blood, sweat, fat, tears, grease, saliva, nasal mucus, synovial fluid, urine."

Just as if there were a double-mouthed provision bag full of various kinds of grain such as hill paddy, paddy, green gram, cow-peas, sesamum, and husked rice, and a man with sound eyes, having opened that bag, were to take stock of the contents thus: This is hill paddy, this is paddy, this is green gram, this is cow-pea, this is sesamum, this is husked rice. Just so, monks, a monk reflects on this very body enveloped by the skin and full of manifold impurity, from the soles up, and from the top of the head-hair down. . . .

Thus he lives contemplating the body in the body. . . .

And further, monks, a monk reflects on this very body, however it be placed or disposed, by way of the material elements: "There are in this body the element of earth, the element of water, the element of fire, the element of wind."

Just as if, monks, a clever cow-butcher or his apprentice, having slaughtered a cow and divided it into portions, should be sitting at the junction of four high roads, in the same way, a monk reflects on this very body, as it is placed or disposed, by way of the material elements: "There are in this body the elements of earth, water, fire and wind."

Thus he lives contemplating the body in the body. . . .

And further, monks, as if a monk sees a body dead one, two, or three days; swollen, blue and festering, thrown in the charnel ground, he then applies this perception to his own body thus: "Verily, also my own body is of the same nature; such it will become and will not escape it."

And further, monks, as if a monk sees a body thrown in the charnel ground, being eaten by crows, hawks, vultures, dogs, jackals, or by different kinds of worms, he then applies this perception to his own body thus: "Verily, also my own body is of the same nature, such it will become and will not escape it."

And further, monks, as if a monk sees a body thrown in the charnel ground and reduced to a skeleton with some flesh and blood attached to it, held together by the tendons. . . ; reduced to a skeleton, blod-besmeared and without flesh held together by the tendons. . . ; reduced to a skeleton without flesh and blood, held together by the tendons. . . ; reduced to disconnected bones, scattered in all directions—here a bone of the hand, there a bone of the foot, a shin bone, a thigh bone, the pelvis, spine and skull. . . ; reduced to bleached bones of conch-like color. . . ; reduced to bones, more than a year old, lying in a heap. . . ; reduced to bones gone rotten and become dust, he then applies this perception to his own body thus: "Verily, also my own body is of the same nature; such it will become and will not escape it."

Thus he lives contemplating the body in the body. . . .

II THE CONTEMPLATION OF FEELING

And how, monks, does a monk live contemplating feelings in feelings?

Herein, monks, a monk when experiencing a pleasant feeling knows, "I experience a pleasant feeling"; when experiencing a painful feeling, he knows, "I experience a painful feeling"; when experiencing a neither-pleasant-nor-painful feeling, he knows, "I experience a neither-pleasant-nor-painful feeling." When experiencing a pleasant worldly feeling, he knows, "I experience a pleasant worldly feeling"; when experiencing a pleasant spiritual feeling, he knows, "I experience a pleasant spiritual feeling"; when experiencing a painful worldly feeling, he knows, "I experience a painful worldly feeling"; when experiencing a painful spiritual feeling, he knows, "I experience a painful spiritual feeling"; when experiencing a neither-pleasant-nor-painful worldly feeling, he knows, "I experience a neither-pleasant-nor-painful worldly feeling"; when experiencing a neither-pleasant-nor-painful spiritual feeling, he knows, "I experience a neither-pleasant-nor-painful spiritual feeling."

Thus he lives contemplating feelings in feelings internally, or he lives contemplating feelings in feelings externally, or he lives contemplating feelings in feelings internally and externally. He lives contemplating origination-factors in feelings, or he lives contemplating dissolution-factors in feelings, or he lives contemplating origination-and-dissolution factors in feelings. Or his mindfulness is established with the thought, "Feeling exists," to the extent necessary just for knowledge and mindfulness, and he lives detached, and clings to naught in the world. Thus, monks, a monk lives contemplating feelings in feelings.

III THE CONTEMPLATION OF CONSCIOUSNESS

And how, monks, does a monk live contemplating consciousness in consciousness?

Herein, monks, a monk knows the consciousness with lust, as with lust; the consciousness without lust as without lust; the consciousness with hate, as with hate; the consciousness without hate, as without hate; the consciousness with ignorance, as with ignorance; the consciousness without ignorance, as without ignorance; the shrunken state of consciousness as the shrunken state; the distracted state of consciousness as the distracted state; the developed state of consciousness as the developed state; the undeveloped state of consciousness as the undeveloped state; the state of consciousness with some other mental state superior to it, as the state with something mentally higher; the state of consciousness with no other mental state superior to it, as the state with nothing mentally higher; the concentrated state of consciousness as the concentrated state; the unconcentrated state of consciousness as the unconcentrated state; the freed state of consciousness as the freed state; and the unfreed state of consciousness as the unfreed.

Thus he lives contemplating consciousness in consciousness internally, or he lives contemplating consciousness in consciousness externally, or he lives contemplating consciousness in consciousness internally and externally. He lives contemplating origination-factors in consciousness, or he lives contemplating dissolution-factors in consciousness, or he lives contemplating origination-and-dissolution factors in consciousness. Or his mindfulness is established with the thought, "Consciousness exists," to the extent necessary just for knowledge and mindfulness, and he lives detached, and clings to naught in the world. Thus monks, a monk lives contemplating consciousness in consciousness.

IV THE CONTEMPLATION OF MENTAL OBJECTS

And how, monks, does a monk live contemplating mental objects in mental objects?

Herein, monks, a monk lives contemplating mental objects in the mental objects of the five hindrances.

And how, monks, does a monk live contemplating mental objects in the mental objects of the five hindrances?

Herein, monks, when sense-desire is present, a monk knows, "There is sense-desire in me," or when sense-desire is not present, he knows, "There is no sense-desire in me." He knows how the arising of the non-arisen sense-desire comes to be; he knows how the abandoning of the arisen sense-desire comes to be; and he knows how the non-arising in the future of the abandoned sense-desire comes to be.

When anger is present, he knows, "There is anger in me"; or when anger is not present, he knows, "There is no anger in me." He knows how the arising of the non-arisen anger comes to be; he knows how the abandoning of the arisen anger comes to be; and he knows how the non-arising in the future of the abandoned anger comes to be.

When sloth and torpor are present, he knows. . . .

When agitation and worry are present, he knows. . . .

When doubt is present, he knows. . . .

Thus he lives contemplating mental objects in mental objects internally, or he lives contemplating mental objects in mental objects externally, or he lives contemplating mental objects in mental objects internally and externally. He lives contemplating origination-factors in mental objects, or he lives contemplating dissolution-factors in mental objects, or he lives contemplating origination-and-dissolution factors in mental objects. Or his mindfulness is established with the thought, "Mental objects exist," to the extent necessary just for knowledge and mindfulness, and he lives detached, and clings to naught in the world. Thus also, monks, a monk lives contemplating mental objects in the mental objects of the five hindrances.

And further, monks, a monk lives contemplating mental objects in the mental objects of the five aggregates of clinging.

How, monks, does a monk live contemplating mental objects in the mental objects of the five aggregates of clinging?

Herein, monks, a monk thinks, "Thus is form; thus is the arising of form; and thus is the disappearance of form. Thus is feeling; thus is the arising of feeling; and thus is the disappearance of feeling. Thus is perception; thus is the arising of perception; and thus is the disappearance of perception. Thus are formations; thus is the arising of formations; and thus is the disappearance of formations. Thus is consciousness; thus is the arising of consciousness; and thus is the disappearance of consciousness."

Thus he lives contemplating mental objects in mental objects. . . .

And further, monks, a monk lives contemplating mental objects in the mental objects of the six internal and the six external sense-bases.

How, monks, does a monk live contemplating mental objects in the mental objects of the six internal and the six external sense-bases?

Herein, monks, a monk knows, the eye and visual forms, and the fetter that arises dependent on both (the eye and forms); he knows how the arising of the non-arisen fetter comes to be; he knows how the abandoning of the arisen fetter comes to be; and he knows how the non-arising in the future of the abandoned fetter comes to be.

He knows the ear and sounds . . . the nose and smells . . . the tongue and flavors . . . the body and tactual objects . . . the mind and mental objects, and the fetter that arises dependent on both; he knows how the arising of the non-arisen fetter comes to be; he knows how the abandoning of the arisen fetter comes to be; and he knows how the non-arising in the future of the abandoned fetter comes to be.

Thus, monks, the monk lives contemplating mental objects in mental objects. . . .

And further, monks, a monk lives contemplating mental objects in the mental objects of the seven factors of enlightenment. . . .

How, monks, does a monk live contemplating mental objects in the mental objects of the seven factors of enlightenment?

Herein, monks, when the enlightenment-factor of mindfulness is present, the monk knows, "The enlightenment-factor of mindfulness is in me," or when the enlightenment-factor of mindfulness is absent, he knows, "The enlightenment-factor of mindfulness is not in me"; and he knows how the arising of the non-arisen enlightenment-factor of mindfulness comes to be; and how perfection in the development of the arisen enlightenment-factor of mindfulness comes to be.

When the enlightenment-factor of the investigation of mental objects is present, the monk knows, "The enlightenment-factor of the investigation of mental objects is in me"; when the enlightenment-factor of the investigation of mental objects is absent, he knows, "The enlightenment-factor of the investigation of mental objects is not in me"; and he knows how the arising of the non-arisen enlightenment-factor of the investigation of mental objects comes to be, and how perfection in the development of the arisen enlightenment-factor of the investigation of mental objects comes to be.

When the enlightenment-factor of energy is present, he knows. . . .

When the enlightenment-factor of joy is present, he knows. . . .

When the enlightenment-factor of tranquility is present, he knows. . . .

When the enlightenment-factor of concentration is present, he knows. . . .

When the enlightenment-factor of equanimity is present, he knows. . . .

Thus he lives contemplating mental objects in mental objects. . . .

And further, monks, a monk lives contemplating mental objects in the mental objects of the four noble truths.

How, monks, does a monk live contemplating mental objects in the mental objects of the four noble truths?

Herein, monks, a monk knows, "This is suffering," according to reality; he knows, "This is the origin of suffering," according to reality; he knows, "This is the cessation of suffering," according to reality; he knows, "This is the road leading to the cessation of suffering," according to reality.

Thus he lives contemplating mental objects in mental objects. . . .

Verily, monks, whosoever practises these four Foundations of Mindfulness in this manner. . . ; then one of these two fruits may be expected by him: Highest Knowledge here and now, or if some remainder of clinging is yet present, the state of non-returning.

Because of this was it said: "This is the only way, monks, for the purification of beings, for the overcoming of sorrow and lamentation, for the destruction of suffering and grief, for reaching the right path, for the attainment of Nibbana, namely the four Foundations of Mindfulness."

Thus spoke the Blessed One. Satisfied, the monks approved of his words.

Abridged from the translation of Nyanasatta Thera

REMARKS ON THE TRADITION OF MINDFULNESS

For the follower of the buddhadharma, there is a need for great emphasis on the practice of meditation. One must see the straightforward logic that mind is the cause of confusion and that, transcending mind, one attains the enlightened state. This can only take place through the practice of meditation. Buddha himself experienced this, working on his own mind; and what he learned has been handed down to us, notably in the *Satipatthana Sutta*, which expounds the beginning of the way of Buddhist meditation—through mindfulness.

It is extremely important to begin at the beginning, rather than entertaining oneself with colorful advanced pursuits. As the great Indian teacher Atisa Dipankara, who taught in Tibet in the eleventh century, said, "Without perfect *samatha* [mindfulness], one might meditate diligently for a thousand years without attaining samadhi." Since mindfulness is the foundation stone of Buddhist practice, common to all traditions and sects, and since the teaching of the Buddha as expressed in the *Satipatthana Sutta* preserves the basic inspiration from which that practice has arisen, we present it here in this number of *Garuda* as the first main piece, the crown jewel of the teaching of mindfulness.

Mindfulness is the beginning of a meditative discipline which leads to greater awareness. Fundamental to this meditative discipline as transmitted through the Kagyu order of Tibetan Buddhism are the sayings known as the "four dharmas of Gampopa." Gampopa (1079-1153) founded the monastic tradition of the Kagyu order. His four dharmas are:

> May my mind follow the dharma.
>
> May my practice win success on the path.
>
> In following the path, may confusion be clarified.
>
> May confusion be transformed into wisdom.

The first dharma entails training the mind so that it becomes dharma, which means that all its activities arise from mindfulness. To begin with, mental activities are only reminders of dharma, reminders of openness. Then, when the mind has become dharma, its natural movement is the journey of the spiritual path, which is the discipline of openness. This journey clarifies confusion. When confusion is clarified, its energy is transmuted into the energy of wisdom.

The four dharmas of Gampopa express the *triyana* or triple-vehicle nature of the Buddhist path, on which, with the practice of mindfulness, we are only at the beginning. Mindfulness is the level of the hinayana, in which one takes care to follow the path. The mahayana begins with the realization that one's mind is the path and therefore its spontaneous activities are riches for oneself and others. Generosity and clarity arise as one. Vajrayana or tantra departs from the point where whatever arises in the mind is experienced as the play of wisdom and skillful means, subtly yet powerfully working towards the enlightenment of all sentient beings.

The *Satipatthana Sutta,* abridged here owing to considerations of space, belongs to the theravadin teaching and preserves the flavor of early Buddhism. According to tradition, Buddha's disciple whose question was the occasion of this discourse was the bodhisattva Chandrakumara. Gampopa is said to have been an incarnation of Chandrakumara. Thus the oral transmission concerning the foundations of mindfulness is a powerful current in the Kagyu heritage which I am presenting.

The following exposition of mind and the foundations of mindfulness, taken from my talks, does not correspond specifically to the letter of Buddha's discourse. Rather it is taken from the treasury of the living oral teaching, which seeks to make Buddha's instruction palpable to the contemporary practitioner in whatever age. This particular teaching seeks to open the way of mindfulness by showing the essence of each of the four foundations, the inner key to its practice. Thus the mindfulness of body of the *Sutta* is seen through the understanding of the psychosomatic body and the sense of being. The *Sutta's* mindfulness of feeling develops the intimacy of the mindfulness of life. The core of the mindfulness of mind is expounded as the effort which prepares the ground for a flash of abstract mind. The mindfulness of mental objects becomes the mindfulness of the projection of the world in terms of the total simplicity of single acts of mind.

FOUNDATIONS OF MINDFULNESS

Mindfulness is a basic approach to the spiritual journey that is common to all traditions of Buddhism. But before we begin to look at that approach to spirituality, we should have some idea of what is meant by spirituality itself. Some say that spirituality is a way of attaining a better kind of happiness, transcendental happiness. Others see it as a benevolent way to develop power over others. Still others say the point of spirituality is to acquire power and magical energies so we can change our bad world into a good world or purify the world through miracles. It seems that any of these points of view is irrelevant to the Buddhist approach. According to the buddhadharma, spirituality is relating with the working basis of our existence, which is our state of mind.

There is a problem with our basic life, our basic being. This problem is that we are involved in a continual struggle to survive, to maintain our position. We are continually trying to grasp onto some solid image of ourselves. And then we have to defend that particular fixed conception. So there is warfare, there is confusion, there is passion and aggression; there are all kinds of conflicts. From the Buddhist point of view, the true development of spirituality is cutting through our basic fixation, that clinging, that stronghold of something-or-other which is known as ego.

In order to do that we have to find out what ego is. What is this all about? Who are we? We have to look into our already existing state of mind. And we have to understand what practical step we can take to do that. We are not involved here in a metaphysical discussion about the purpose of life and meaning of spirituality on an abstract level. We are looking at this question from the point of view of a working situation. We need to find some simple thing we can do by way of embarking on the spiritual path.

People have a lot of difficulty in beginning on spiritual practice, because they put a lot of energy into looking for the best and easiest way to get into it. We might have to change our attitude and give up looking for the best or the easiest way. Actually, there is no choice. Whatever approach we take, we will have to deal with what we are already. We have to look at who we are. According to the Buddhist tradition, the working basis of the path and the energy involved in the path is the mind, our own mind that we have working in us all the time.

Spirituality is based on mind. In Buddhism, mind is the distinguishing mark of sentient beings as opposed to rocks or trees or bodies of water. That which possesses discriminating awareness, that which possesses a sense of duality—grasps or rejects something external— that is mind. Fundamentally, it is that which can associate with an "other," any "something" perceived as different from the perceiver. That is the definition of mind. The traditional Tibetan phrase defining mind—*yul la sems pena sems*—means precisely that: "That which can think of the other, the projection, is mind."

So by mind we mean something very specific. It is not just something very vague and creepy inside our head or heart, something that just happens as part of the way the wind blows and the grass grows. Rather it is something very concrete. It contains perception, perception that is very uncomplicated, very basic, very precise. Mind develops its particular nature as that perception begins to linger on something other than oneself. That is the mental trick that constitutes mind. The tricky part is that mind makes the fact of perceiving something else stand for the existence of oneself. In fact, it should be the opposite: since the perception starts from oneself, the logic should be: "I exist, therefore the other exists."

But somehow the hypocrisy of mind is developed to such an extent that it lingers on the other as a way of getting the feedback that it itself exists, which is an erroneous belief fundamentally. It is the fact that the existence of self is questionable that motivates the trick of duality.

This is the mind that is our working basis for the practice of meditation and the development of awareness. But mind is something more than the process of confirming self by the dualistic lingering on the other. Mind also includes what are known as emotions, which are the highlights of mental states. Mind cannot exist without emotions. Pure daydreaming and pure discursive thoughts alone are not enough. Those alone would be too boring. The dualistic trick would wear too thin. So we tend to create waves of emotion which go up and down—passion, aggression, ignorance, pride—all kinds of emotions. We create them deliberately at the beginning, as a game of trying to prove to ourself that we exist. But eventually the game becomes a hassle; it becomes more than a game and forces us to challenge ourselves more than we intended. It is like a hunter who, for the sport of practicing his shooting, decides to shoot one leg of a deer at a time. But the deer runs very fast, and it appears it might get away altogether. This becomes a total challenge to the hunter who rushes after the deer, now trying to kill it completely, to shoot it in the heart. So the hunter has been challenged and feels defeated by his own game.

Emotions are like this. They are not a requirement for survival; they are a game we developed that went wrong at some point, went sour. In the face of this predicament we feel terribly frustrated and absolutely helpless. Such frustration causes some people to fortify their relationship to the "other" by creating "god" or other projections such as saviors, gurus, mahatmas and so on. We create all kinds of projections as henchmen, hitmen, to enable us to re-dominate our territory. The implicit sense is that through our paying homage to such great beings, they will function as our helpers, as our guarantors of ground.

So we have created a rather neat world. It is bittersweet. Things are amusing, but at the same time, not so amusing. Sometimes things seem terribly funny, but, on the other hand, terribly sad. Life has the quality of a game of ours that has trapped us. The set-up of mind has created the whole thing. We might complain about the government or the economy of the country or the prime rate of interest, but those factors are secondary. The original process at the root of the problems is the competitiveness that we create within ourselves. We have already set up that primeval competitiveness of seeing ourselves only as a reflection of the other. Problematic situations arise automatically as expressions of that. They are our own production, our own neat work. And that is what is called mind.

According to the Buddhist tradition, there are eight types of consciousness and fifty-two types of conceptions and all kinds of other aspects of mind, about which we do not have to go into details. All are largely based on the primeval dualistic approach. There are the spiritual aspects and the psychological aspects and all sorts of other aspects. All are bound up in the realm of duality, which is ego.

As far as meditation practice is concerned, in meditation we work on *this* thing, rather than trying to sort out the problem from the outside. We work on the projector rather than the projection. We turn inward, instead of trying to sort out external problems of A, B, and C. We work on the creator of duality rather than the creation. That is beginning at the beginning.

There are three main aspects of "this," according to the Buddhist tradition, called in Tibetan *sems, rigpa* and *yid.* The basic mind, the simple capacity for duality we have already described, is *sems. Rigpa* literally means "intelligence" or "brightness." In colloquial Tibetan, if you say that somebody has *rigpa*, it means he is a clever, sharp fellow. This sharpness of *rigpa* is a kind of side function that develops from the basic mind, *sems,* a kind of lawyer's mentality that everybody develops. It looks at a problem from various different angles and analyzes the possibilities of different ways of approaching it. It looks at the problem in every possible way, inside-out and outside-in.

The third aspect, *yid,* is considered a sense consciousness. Traditionally it is classified as the sixth sense consciousness. There is sight, smell, taste, hearing, touch, and the sixth is the *yid. Yid* is not exactly mind in the sense of *sems,* but it is more mental sensitivity. It is associated with the heart and is a kind of balancing factor which acts as a switchboard in relation to the other five sense consciousnesses. When you see a sight and you hear a sound at the same time, the sight and sound are synchronized to constitute aspects of a single event by the sixth sense. It does a kind of automatic synchronization job, or automatic computerization of the whole process of sense experience. You can see, smell, hear, taste and feel all at the same time and all of those inputs are coherently workable. They make sense to you because of *yid.*

So *yid* is a sort of central-headquarters switchboard, which coordinates our experience into a coherent whole. In some sense it is the most important one of all the three aspects of mind. It is not as intelligent in the sense of manipulation as *sems. Sems* has something of a political attitude towards one's relationship with the world; it is somewhat strategy oriented. The sixth sense is more domestic in function. It just tries to maintain the coordination of experience so that all information comes through efficiently, so that there is no problem of being out of communication with anything that is going on. On the other hand *rigpa*, which is the intelligence, the research worker, as it were, in this administration of mind, takes an overall view of one's whole situation. It surveys the relationship between mind and the sixth sense and tries to search out all the possibilities of where things are going wrong, where things might go wrong, where things have gone wrong, how things could be put right. This research worker does not have the power actually to take action on the level of external relations. It is more like an advisor to the state department.

These three principles of *sems*, *rigpa* and *yid* are the most important for us to be aware of at this point. Many other aspects of mind are described in the traditional literature, but these three will suffice for our present understanding.

We should consider this understanding not so much as something that we have been told and therefore we should believe in. The experience described here can actually be felt personally. It can be worked on, related to. A certain part of our experience is organized by our basic mind, a certain part by our sixth sense, and a certain part by our intelligence. In order to understand the basic functions of mindfulness-awareness practice, I think it is very important for us to understand and realize these complexities of our mind.

What we usually do when we get hassled while meditating and feel we cannot sit anymore is to put all of these aspects of mind into one bag and blame our frustration on "this thing." We are frustrated, we feel completely wretched; we feel there are no alternatives and are just sorry for ourselves. Or else we look for alternatives: we go to the movies or buy chewing gum or whatever. But somehow life is not as simple as that. It is not as simple as thinking that "this thing," taken as a lump, is a bad thing; nor can we get away from the basic hassle by going to the movies or buying chewing gum. What is necessary is to make friends with ourselves, to work openly with our basic situation.

There is a gigantic world of mind that exists to which we are almost totally unexposed. This whole world—this tent and this microphone, this light, this grass, the very pair of spectacles that we are wearing—is made by our mind. Everybody's mind made this up, put these things together. Every bolt and nut was put in by somebody-or-other's mind. This whole world is mind's world, the product of mind. This is needless to say; I am sure everybody knows this. But we might remind ourselves of it so that we realize that meditation is not an exclusive activity which means forgetting this world and getting into something else. By meditating, we are dealing with that very mind that devised our eyeglasses and put the lenses in the rims, and that very mind that put up this tent. Our coming here is the product of our mind. Each of us has different mental manifestations which permit others to identify us and say, "This guy is named so-and-so, this girl is named so-and-so." We can be identified as individuals because we have different mental approaches, which also shape the expressions of our physical features. Our physical characteristics are a part of our mental activity as well. So this is a living world, mind's world. Realizing this, working with mind is no longer a remote or mysterious thing to do. It is no longer dealing with something that is hidden or somewhere else. Mind is right here. Mind is hanging out in the world. It is an open secret.

The method for beginning to relate directly with mind, taught by Lord Buddha and in use for the past 2,500 years, is the practice of mindfulness. There are four aspects to this practice, traditionally known as the four foundations of mindfulness.

Mindfulness of Body

The first foundation of mindfulness is mindfulness of body. The practice of mindfulness of body is connected with the need for a sense of being, a sense of groundedness.

To begin with, there is some problem about what we understand by "body." We have a body. We sit on chairs or on the ground; we eat; we sleep; we wear clothes. But the body that we relate with in going through these activities is questionable. Is it the unconditional body, free from any conceptualizations; or is it a body constituted by conceptualizations? According to the tradition, the body we have is what is known as the "mind-body" or psychosomatic body. It is largely based on projections and concepts of body. This mind-body contrasts with the enlightened person's sense of body, which might be called "body-body." This is just simple and straightforward. There is a direct relationship with the earth. As for us, we do not actually have a relationship with the earth. We have some relationship with our body, but it is very uncertain and erratic. We flicker back and forth between body and something else—fantasies, ideas. That seems to be our basic situation.

Even though the psychosomatic body is constituted by projections of body, it can be quite a solid one in terms of those projections. We have expectations concerning the existence of our body, therefore we have to refuel it, entertain it, wash it. What we are involved in with this psychosomatic body is a sense of being. For instance, at this moment you feel that you are sitting on the ground. You have your sense of being in terms of your body resting on the ground. Your buttocks are resting on the earth, therefore you can extend your legs and lean back a little so you have less strain on your body. You have some sense of relaxation as opposed to how it would be if everybody was standing or if just you were standing—standing on your feet, standing on your toes or standing on your palms. In contrast to these postures, this posture that you are adopting at the moment seems to be an agreeable one, in fact it is one of the most congenial postures that one could ever think of. So being in this posture you can relax and listen, listen to something other than the demands of your body.

Sitting down now, you feel somewhat settled. On the other hand, if the ground was very damp, for instance, you would not feel so settled. Then you would begin to perch on the ground, like a bird on a branch. This is another matter altogether. If you are intensely concerned with some event about to happen, if you are worried about some encounter you are about to have—if you are being interviewed for a job by some executive, for example— you don't really sit on your chair, you perch on it. Perching happens when some demand is being made on you and you feel less of your body and more of your tension and nervousness. It involves a very different sense of body and of being than just sitting as you are doing now.

Right now you are sitting on the ground and you are so completely sitting down that you have been able to shift gears from that and turn on your tape recorders and even start taking notes. You do not regard that as doing two things at once, but you sit there, you have totally flopped, so to speak, and having done that you can turn to your other perceptions—listening, looking and so on. A body situation of having settled and so being able to turn to something else is involved.

But that process of your sitting here at this point is not actually very much a matter of your body *per se* sitting on the ground, but far more a matter of your psychosomatic body sitting on the ground. Somehow sitting on the ground here gives you an idea—particularly all facing in one direction, towards the speaker; and being underneath the roof of the tent; being attracted to the light that is focused on the stage—all this creates a certain style of participation, which is the condition of your psychosomatic body. You are somewhat involved in sitting *per se,* but at the same time you are not. Mind is doing it, concept is doing it. Your mind is shaping the situation in accordance with your body. Your mind is sitting on the ground. Your mind is taking notes. Your mind is wearing glasses. Your mind has such-and-such a hairdo; your mind is wearing such-and-such clothes. Everyone is creating a portrait of themselves. The body exists; therefore mind activity takes place and creates the world according to the body situation, but largely out of contact with it. That is the psychosomatic process.

Mindfulness of body brings this all-pervasive mind-imitating-body activity into the practice of meditation. The practice of meditation has to take into account the mind continually shaping itself into body*like* attitudes. Consequently, since the time of Buddha, sitting meditation has been recommended and practiced and it has proved to be the best way of dealing with this situation. The basic technique that goes with sitting meditation is working with the breath. You identify with the breath, particularly with the outbreath. The inbreath is just a gap, a space. During the inbreath you just wait. So you breathe out and then you dissolve and then there is a gap. Breathe out . . . dissolve . . . gap. An openness, an expansion can take place constantly that way.

Mindfulness plays a very important role in this technique. Mindfulness, in this case, means that when you sit and meditate, you actually do sit. You actually do sit as far as the psychosomatic body is concerned. You feel the ground, body, breath, temperature. You don't try specifically to watch and keep track of what is going on. You don't try to formalize the sitting situation and make it into some special activity that you are performing. You just do sit. And then you begin to feel that there is some sense of groundedness. This is not particularly a product of being deliberate, but is more the force of the actual fact of being there. So you sit. And you sit. And you breathe. And you sit and you breathe. Sometimes you think, but still you are thinking sitting thoughts. The psychosomatic body is sitting, so your thoughts have a flat bottom.

You go on and on sitting. And then somehow you have a sense, a feeling, that you have done something. That is one of the most important characteristics of mindfulness—that you feel you are actually doing something. In this case you feel that you are taking part in some particular experience or project that has a flat bottom. It is not ball-like, it does not have wings, but psychosomatically it actually has a flat bottom.

That mindfulness of body is connected with the earth. It is an openness which has a base, a foundation. A quality of expansive awareness develops through mindfulness of body,

a sense of being settled and therefore being able to afford to open out.

Going along with this mindfulness requires a great deal of trust. Probably the beginning meditator will not be able simply to rest there, but will feel the need for a change. I remember someone who had just finished a retreat telling me how she sat and felt her body and felt grounded. But then she thought immediately how she should be doing something else. And she went on to tell me how the right book "just jumped in my lap" and she started to read. At that point you don't have a solid base anymore. Your mind is beginning to grow little wings. The mindfulness of body has to do with trying to remain human, rather than becoming animals or flies or etheric beings. It means just trying to remain a human being, an ordinary human being.

The basic starting point for this is this solidness, groundedness. When you sit, you actually sit. Even your floating thoughts begin to sit on their own bottoms. There are no particular problems. You have a sense of solidness, groundedness and, at the same time, a sense of being.

Without this particular foundation of mindfulness, the rest of your meditation practice could be very airy-fairy—vacillating back and forth, trying this and trying that. You could be constantly tiptoeing the surface of the universe, not actually getting a foothold anywhere. You could become an eternal hitchhiker. So with this first technique you develop some basic solidness. In the mindfulness of body, there is a sense of finding some home ground.

Mindfulness of Life

The application of mindfulness has to be precise. If we cling to our practice, that creates fundamental stagnation. Therefore, in our application of the techniques of mindfulness, we must be aware of the fundamental tendency to cling, to survive. We come to this in the second foundation of mindfulness, which is the mindfulness of survival or life. Since we are dealing with the context of meditation, we encounter this tendency in the form of clinging to the meditative state. We experience the meditative state and it is momentarily tangible, but in the same moment we experience it, it is dissolving. Going along with this process means developing a sense of letting go of awareness as well as of contacting it. This is the basic technique of this second foundation of mindfulness, which could be described as "touch and go." You are there—present, mindful—and then you let go.

The general misunderstanding that exists is that the meditative state of mind has to be captured and then nursed and cherished. That is definitely the wrong approach. If you try to domesticate your mind through meditation, try to possess it by holding onto the meditative state, the clear result will be regression on the path, a loss of freshness and spontaneity. If you try to hold on without lapse all the time, then maintaining your awareness begins to become a domestic hassle. It becomes like painfully going through housework. There will be an underlying sense of resentment and the practice of meditation will become confusing. You will begin to develop a love-hate relationship towards your practice, in which your concept of it seems good, but, at the same time, the demand this rigid concept makes on you is too painful.

So the technique of the mindfulness of life is based on "touch and go." The awareness or the object of awareness is developed and you focus your attention on it. But then, in the same moment, you disown it and go on. What is needed here is some sense of confidence, confidence that you do not have to securely own your mind, but can tune into its process spontaneously.

Mindfulness of life relates to the clinging tendency not only in connection with the meditative state, but, even more importantly, on the raw level of anxiety about survival that manifests in us constantly, second by second, minute by minute. You breathe for survival, you lead life for survival. The feeling is constantly present that you are trying to protect yourself from death. For the practical purposes of the second foundation, instead of regarding this survival mentality as something negative, instead of relating to it as ego-clinging as is done in the abstract philosophical overview of Buddhism, this particular practice switches the logic around. In the second foundation, the survival struggle is regarded as a steppingstone in the practice of meditation. Whenever you have the sense of the survival instinct functioning, that can be transmuted into a sense of being, a sense of having already survived. Mindfulness becomes a basic acknowledgement of existing. This does not have the flavor of "Thank God, I have survived." Instead, it is more an objective, impartial "I am alive, I am here, sobeit."

At this point, meditation becomes an actual part of life, rather than just a practice or exercise. It becomes inseparable from the instinct to live that accompanies all our experience. That instinct to live can be seen as containing awareness, meditation, mindfulness. It constantly tunes us in to what is happening. So the life force that keeps us alive and that manifests itself continually in our stream of consciousness, itself becomes the practice of mindfulness. Such mindfulness brings clarity, skill and intelligence. Experience is brought from the framework of intense psychosomatic confusion into that of the real body, because we are simply tuning into what is *already* happening instead of projecting anything further.

Since mindfulness is part of our stream of consciousness, the practice of meditation cannot be regarded as something alien, an emulation of some picturesque yogi who has a fixation on meditating all the time. Seen from the point of view of the mindfulness of life, meditation is the total experience of any living being who has the instinct to survive. Therefore, meditating, developing mindfulness, should not be regarded as a minority-group activity or some specialized, eccentric pursuit. It is a wide-world approach which relates to all experience—it is tuning into life.

Frequently people undertake the practice of meditation with a sense of purity or austerity. They somehow feel that by meditating they are doing the right thing and they feel like good boys and good girls. Not only are they doing the right thing, but they are also getting away from the ugly world. They are becoming pure; they are renouncing the world and becoming like the great yogis of the past. They don't actually live and meditate in caves but they can regard the corner of the room that they have arranged for meditation as a cave. They can close their eyes and feel that they are meditating in a cave in the mountains. That kind of imagination makes them feel rather good. It feels fitting; it feels clean and secure.

There is this strong tendency to isolate the practice of meditation from our actual living situation. We build up all kinds of extraneous concepts and images about it. It is satisfying to regard meditation as austere and above life. But mindfulness of life steers us in just the opposite direction. The approach of mindfulness of life is that if you are meditating in a room, you are meditating in a room. You don't regard the room as a cave. If you are breathing, you are breathing, rather than convincing yourself you are a motionless rock. You keep your eyes open and simply let yourself be where you are. There are no imaginations involved with this approach. You just go through with your situation as it is. If your meditation place is in a rich setting, just be in the midst of it. If it is in a simple setting, just be in the midst of that. You are not trying to get away from anywhere to anywhere else. You are tuning in simply and directly to your process of life. This practice is the essence of here and now.

You do not tune in as part of trying to live further. You do not approach mindfulness as a further elaboration of the survival instinct. Rather you just see the sense of survival as it is taking place in you already. You are here; you are living; let it be that way—that is mindfulness. Your heart pulsates and you breathe. All kinds of things are happening at once in you. Let mindfulness work with that, let that be mindfulness, let every beat of your heart be mindfulness itself, let every breath. You do not have to breathe specially; your breath *is* an expression of mindfulness. If you approach meditation in this way, it becomes very personal and very direct.

Having such an outlook and such a relationship with the practice of meditation brings enormous strength, enormous energy and power. But this only comes if your relation to the present situation is accurate. Otherwise there is no strength because you are apart from the energy of that situation. The accuracy of mindfulness, on the other hand, brings not only strength, but a sense of dignity and delight. This is simply because you are doing something that is applicable that very moment. And you are doing it without any implications or motives. It is direct and right on the point.

But, again it is necessary to say, once you have that experience of the presence of life, don't hang onto it. Just touch and go. Touch that presence of life being lived, then go. You do not have to ignore it. "Go" does not mean that you have to turn your back on the experience and shut yourself off from it, it means just to be in it without further analysis and without further reinforcement. Holding onto life, or trying to reassure yourself that it is so, has the sense of death rather than life. It is only because you have that sense of death that you want to make sure that you are alive. You would like to have an insurance policy. But if you feel that you are alive, that is good enough. You do not have to make sure that you actually do breathe, that you actually can be seen. You do not have to check up to be sure you have a shadow. Just living is enough without reassuring yourself that you are living. If you don't stop to make sure, living becomes very clearcut, very alive and very precise.

So mindfulness here does not mean pushing yourself to anything or hanging onto anything. It means allowing yourself to be there in the very moment of what is happening in your living process and then letting go.

Mindfulness of Effort

The next foundation of mindfulness is mindfulness of effort. The idea of effort is apparently problematical. Effort would seem to be at odds with the sense of being that arises from mindfulness of body. Also pushing of any kind does not have an obvious place in the touch-and-go technique of the mindfulness of life. In either case, deliberate, heavyhanded

effort would seem to endanger the open precision of the process of mindfulness. Still we cannot expect proper mindfulness to develop without any exertion on our part. Effort is necessary. But in order to develop some notion of right effort, we have to first consider what we mean by effort.

One kind of effort is purely oriented towards the achievement of a result. There is a sense of struggle and pushing, egged on by the sense of a goal. Such an effort picks up momentum and begins to thrive on its own speed. This is effort in the manner of the run of a roadrunner. Another approach to effort is fraught with a sense of tremendous meaning-fulness. There is no sense of uplift or inspiration in the work. Instead there is a strong feeling of being dutiful. You just slog along, slowly and surely, trying to chew through your obligations in the manner of a worm in a tree.

Neither of these kinds of effort have a sense of openness or precision. The traditional Buddhist analogy for right effort is the walk of an elephant or tortoise. The elephant or tortoise moves along surely, unstoppably, with great dignity. Like the worm, it is not excitable. But the worm just bites whatever comes in front of its mouth and chews through. The channel that its belly passes through is its total space. The tortoise or elephant has a panoramic view of the ground it is treading. Though it is serious and slow, because of its ability to survey the ground, there is a sense of playfulness and intelligence in its movement.

In the case of meditation, trying to develop an inspiration that will cause us to forget our pain and make our practice thrive on a sense of continual accomplishment is quite immature. On the other hand, too much solemnity and dutifulness creates a lifeless and narrow outlook and a stale psychological environment. The style of right effort, as taught by Buddha, is serious but not too serious. It takes advantage of the natural flow of instinct to bring the wandering mind constantly back to the mindfulness of breathing.

The crucial point in the bringing-back process is that it is not necessary to go through deliberate stages of preparing to do it, then getting a hold on our attention and then dragging it back to the breathing as if we were trying to drag a naughty child back from doing something terrible. It is not a question of forcing the mind back to some particular object, but of bringing it back down from the dreamworld into reality. You are breathing, you are sitting. That is what you are doing and you should be doing that completely, fully, wholeheartedly.

There is a kind of technique or trick here that is extremely effective and extremely useful, not only for sitting meditation, but also in daily life, for meditation in action. The way of coming back is through what we might call the "abstract watcher." This watcher is just simple self-consciousness, without aim or goal. When we encounter anything, the first flash which takes place is the bare sense of duality, separateness. On that basis, we begin to evaluate, pick and choose, make decisions, execute our will. The abstract watcher is just the basic sense of separateness, just plain cognition of being there before any of the rest develops. Instead of condemning this self-consciousness as dualistic, we take advantage of this tendency in our psychological system as the basis of the mindfulness of effort. The experience is just a sudden flash of the watcher's being *there*. At that point we don't think, "I must get back to the breath," or "I must try and get away from these thoughts." We don't have to entertain a deliberate and logical movement of mind which repeats to itself the purpose of sitting practice. There is just suddenly a general sense that something is happening here and now, and we are brought back. Abruptly, immediately, without a name, without the application of any kind of concept, we have a quick glimpse of changing the tone. That is the core of the mindfulness-of-effort practice.

One of the reasons that ordinary effort becomes so dreary and stagnant is that our intention always develops a verbalization. Subconsciously, we actually verbalize: "I must go and help so-and-so because it is half-past one." Or, "This is a good thing for me to do; it is good for me to perform this duty." Any kind of sense of duty we might have is always verbalized, though the speed of conceptual mind is so great we may not even notice the verbalization. Still the contents of the verbalization are clearly felt. This verbalization pins the effort to a fixed frame of reference, which makes it extremely tiresome. In contrast, this abstract effort we are talking about flashes in a fraction of a second, without any name or any idea with it. It is just a jerk, a sudden change of course that does not define its destination. The rest of the effort is just like a tortoise's walk, step-by-step, going slowly, observing the situation around us.

You could call this abstract self-consciousness "leap" if you like, or "jerk" or "sudden reminder"; or you could call it "amazement." Sometimes it could also be felt as panic, unconditioned panic, because of the change of course—something comes to us and changes our whole course. If we work with this sudden jerk, and do so with no effort in the effort, then effort becomes self-existing. It stands on its own two feet, so to speak, rather than needing another effort to trigger it off. If the latter were the case, effort would have to be deliberately manufactured, which runs counter to the whole sense of meditation. Then, once you have had that sudden instant of mindfulness, the idea is not to try to maintain it. You should not hold onto it or try to cultivate it. Don't entertain the messenger. Don't nurse the reminder. Get back to meditation. Get into the message.

This kind of effort is extremely important. That sudden flash is a key to all Buddhist meditation, from the level of basic mindfulness to the highest levels of tantra. Such mindfulness of effort could definitely be considered the most important aspect of mindfulness practice. Mindfulness of body creates the general setting; it brings meditation into the psychosomatic set-up of our life. Mindfulness of life makes meditation practice personal and intimate. Mindfulness of effort makes meditation workable. It connects the foundations of mindfulness to the path, to the spiritual journey. It is like the wheel of a chariot, which makes the connection between the chariot and the road, or like the oar of a boat. It actualizes the practice, makes it move, proceed.

But we have a problem here. Mindfulness of effort cannot be deliberately manufactured. On the other hand, it is not enough just to hope that a flash will come to us and we will be reminded. We cannot just leave it up to "that thing" to happen to us. We have to set some kind of general alarm system, so to speak, or prepare a general atmosphere. There must be a background of discipline which sets the tone of the sitting practice. Effort is important on this level also, effort in the sense of not having the faintest indulgence towards any form of entertainment. We have to give something up. Unless we give up our reservations about taking the practice seriously, it is virtually impossible to have that kind of instantaneous effort dawn on us. So it is extremely important to have respect for the practice, a sense of appreciation, a willingness to work hard.

Once we do have a sense of commitment to relating with things as they actually are, that opens the way to the flash which reminds us—*that, that, that*. "That what?" does not apply any more. Just *that*, which triggers an entirely new state of consciousness, which brings us back automatically to mindfulness of breathing or a general sense of being.

We work hard not being diverted into entertainment. Still in some sense we can enjoy the very boring situation of the practice of sitting meditation. We can actually appreciate not having lavish resources of entertainment available. Because of having already included our boredom and ennui, we have nothing to run away from and we feel completely secure and grounded.

This basic sense of appreciation is another aspect of the background that makes it possible for the spontaneous flash of the reminder to occur more easily. This is said to be like falling in love. When we are in love with someone, somehow or other, because our whole attitude is open toward that person, we get a very sudden flash—not of the person by name or a concept of what the person looks like—those are afterthoughts. We get an abstract flash of our lover being *that*. A flash of *that* comes into our mind first. Then we might ponder on it, elaborate it, enjoy our daydreams about it. But all this happens afterwards. The flash is primeval.

Openness always brings that kind of result. Another traditional analogy that has been used is that of the hunter. The hunter does not have to think of a stag or a mountain goat or a bear or any specific animal, but he is looking for *that*. When he walks and hears some sound, senses some subtle possibility, he does not think of what animal he is going to find, just the feeling of *that* comes up. Anybody in any kind of complete involvement, on the hunter's level, the lover's level, or the meditator's level, has that kind of openness which brings about sudden flashes, an almost magical sensation of thatness, without a name, without concept, without idea. This is the instant of effort, concentrated effort, and awareness follows after that. Having disowned that sudden experience, awareness comes very slowly and settles back to the earthy reality of just being there.

Mindfulness of Mind

Often mindfulness is referred to as watchfulness. But that should not give the impression that mindfulness means watching something happening. Mindfulness means being watchful, rather than watching something. This implies a process of intelligent alertness, rather than the mechanical business of simply observing what happens. Particularly the fourth foundation, which is mindfulness of mind, has qualities of an aroused intelligence operating. The intelligence of the fourth foundation is a sense of lighthandedness. If you open the windows and doors of a room the right amount, you can maintain the interior feeling of the roomness and, at the same time, have the freshness from outside. Mindfulness of mind brings that same kind of intelligent balance.

Without mind and its conflicts, we cannot meditate or develop balance, or develop anything at all for that matter. Therefore, conflicts that arise from mind are regarded as a necessary part of the process of mindfulness. But at the same time, those conflicts have to be controlled, enough so that we can come back to our mindfulness of breathing. A balance has to be maintained. There has to be a certain discipline so that we are neither totally lost in daydream, nor missing the freshness and openness that comes from not holding our attention too tightly. This balance is the state of wakefulness, mindfulness.

People with different temperaments bring different approaches to the practice of meditation. Some people are extremely orthodox, in fact dictatorial, with themselves. Other people are extraordinarily loose. They just, so to speak, hang out in the meditation posture and let everything happen. Other people struggle back and forth between those two extremes, not knowing exactly what to do. How one approaches the sitting situation will depend on different moods and different types of people, obviously. But always a certain sense of accuracy is required, and a certain sense of freedom is required.

The meaning of mindfulness of mind is being with your mind. When you sit and meditate, you are there, you are being with your mind. You are being with your body, with your sense of life or survival, with your sense of effort. And at the same time you are being with your mind. You are being there. Mindfulness of mind suggests a sense of presence and a sense of accuracy in terms of being there. You are there, therefore you can't miss yourself. If you are not there, then you might miss yourself. But that also would be a doubletake: If you realize you are not there, that means you are there. That brings you back to where you are. Back to square one.

The whole process is very simple, actually. Unfortunately, explaining the simplicity takes a lot of vocabulary, a lot of grammar, and yards and yards of recording tape. However, it is a very simple matter. And that matter concerns you and your world. Nothing else. It does not particularly concern enlightenment and does not particularly concern metaphysical comprehension. In fact, this simple matter does not particularly concern the next minute, or the minute before. It only concerns the very small area where you are.

Really we operate on a very small basis. We think we are great, broadly significant, and that we cover a whole large area. We see ourselves as having a history and a future, and here we are in our "big deal" present. But if we look at ourselves clearly this very moment, we see we are just a grain of sand, just little people concerned only with this little dot that exists which is called "nowness."

We can only operate on one dot at a time and mindfulness of mind approaches our experience in that way. You are there and you approach yourself on the very simple basis of *that*. "That" does not particularly have many dimensions, many perspectives. It is just a simple thing. Relating directly to this little dot of nowness is the right understanding of austerity. And if we work on this basis, it is possible to begin to see the truth of the matter, so to speak; to begin to see what nowness really means.

This experience is very revealing in that it is very personal. This does not mean personal in the sense of petty and mean. The idea is that this experience is your experience. You might be tempted to share it with somebody else, but then it becomes their experience, rather than what you wished for—your-their experience jumbled together. You can never do that. People have different experiences of reality, which cannot be jumbled together. Invaders and dictators of all kinds have tried to make others have their experience, to make a big concoction of minds controlled by one person. That is impossible. Everyone has failed in making that kind of spiritual pizza. So you have to accept that your experience is personal. This personal experience of nowness is very much there and very obviously there. You cannot even throw it away!

In sitting practice or in the awareness practice of everyday life, for that matter, you are not trying to solve a wide array of problems. You are looking at one situation which is very limited. It is so limited that there is even no room to be claustrophobic. If it is not there, it is not there. You missed it. If it is there, it is there. That is the pinpoint of mindfulness of mind, that simplicity of total up-to-dateness, total directness. Mind functions singly. Once. And once. One thing at a time. The practice of mindfulness of mind is to be there with that one-shot perception, constantly. You get a complete picture from which nothing is missing: that is happening, now that is happening, now that is happening. There is no escape. Even if you focus yourself on escaping, that is also a one-shot movement of which you could be mindful. You can be mindful of your escape—of your sexual fantasy or your aggression fantasy.

One thing at a time happens always—in a direct, simple movement of mind. Therefore traditionally in the technique for mindfulness of mind, it is recommended that you be aware of each single-shot perception as mind as thinking, "I am thinking I hear a sound. I am thinking I smell a scent. I am thinking I feel hot. I am thinking I feel cold." Each one of these is a total approach to experience—very precise, very direct—one single movement of mind. Things always happen in that direct way.

Often we tend to think that we are very clever and can get away from that direct nature of things. We feel we can get around that choiceless simplicity by approaching something from the back door, or from above, from the loft. We feel that way we can prove ourselves extremely intelligent and resourceful. We are cunning and shifty. But somehow it does not work. When we think we are approaching something from the backdoor, we do so under the illusion that there is *something else* to approach. But at that moment there is only the backdoorness. That one-shot backdoorness is the totality of what is. We are the backdoor. If we are approaching from the loft downwards, you, me, everybody, all of us are up there. The whole thing is up there, rather than there being something else for us to go down and invade and control. There isn't anything else at all. It is a one-shot deal. That one-shot reality is all there is. Obviously we can make up an illusion. We can imagine that we are conquering the universe by multiplying ourself into hundreds of aspects and personalities, the conquering and the conquered. But that is like the dream state of someone who is actually asleep. There is only the one shot; everything happens only once. There is just that. Therefore mindfulness of mind is applicable.

So meditation practice has to be approached in a very simple and very basic way. That seems to be the only way that can apply to our experience of what we actually are. That way, we do not get into the illusion that we can function as a hundred people at once. When we lose the simplicity we begin to be concerned about ourselves. "While I'm doing this, such-and-such is going to happen. What shall I do?" Thinking that more than *that* is happening, we get involved in hope and fear in relation to all kinds of things that are not actually happening. Really it does not work that way. While we are doing *that*, we are doing that. If something else happens, we are doing something else. But two things could not happen at once. It is easy to imagine that two things are happening at once, because our journey back and forth between the two may be very speedy. But even then we are doing only one thing at a time. We are jumping back and forth, rather than being in two places at once, which is impossible.

The idea of mindfulness of mind is to slow down that fickleness of jumping back and forth. We have to realize that we are not extraordinary mental acrobats. We are not all that well trained. And even an extraordinarily well trained mind could not manage that many things at once, even not two. But because things are very simple and direct, we can focus, be aware, be mindful of one thing at a time. That one-pointedness, that bare attention seems to be the basic point.

It is necessary to take that logic all the way and realize that even bare attention to what we are doing is impossible. If you have bare attention to what you are doing, you have two personalities. One personality is bare attention, the other personality is doing things. Real bare attention is being there all at once. You do not have bare attention *to* what you are doing; you are not mindful *of* what you are doing. That is impossible. Mindfulness is the act as well as the experience happening at the same time. Obviously, you could have an attitude at the beginning, before you get into real mindfulness, that you are willing to be mindful, willing to surrender, willing to discipline yourself, and that would be somewhat dualistic. But then you do the thing, you just do it. It is like the famous Zen saying, "When I eat, I eat; when I sleep, I sleep." You just do it, with absolutely no implication behind what you are doing, not even of mindfulness. When you begin to feel implications of mindfulness, then you are beginning to split yourself. Then you are faced with your resistance, and hundreds of other things begin seemingly to attack you, to bother you. Trying to be mindful by deliberately looking at yourself involves too much watcher. Then you have lost the one-shot simplicity.

Questions and Answers

Question: I don't understand how *sems* works.

Rinpoche: As we have said, *sems* is the equivalent of "mind." But instead of using the word "mind" as a noun, it might be more helpful to think of it as a verb, as in "minding" or "mind your business." *Sems* is an active process, because you cannot have mind without an object of mind. Mind and its object are one process. Mind only functions in relation to a reference point. In other words, you cannot see anything in the dark. The function of sight is to see something that is not darkness, an object, to see in the light. In the same way, the function of mind is to have a reference point, a relative reference point which survives the mind, the minding process. That is happening right now, actually, everywhere.

Q: I was wondering if you could speak a little more about how mind or minding creates the world. Are you talking about creating in the sense that if we are not mindful of the world the world does not exist? I feel you're saying something else besides that.

R: Well, mind is very simple perception—it can only survive on "other." Otherwise it starves to death.

Q: You mean the mind can only exist on things outside of itself?

R: That is right. But there is also the possibility that mind can go too far in that direction. Mind cannot exist on itself alone without the projection of a relative reference point. On the other hand, mind also cannot exist if it is too crowded with projections. That way it also loses its reference point. So mind has to maintain a certain balance. To begin with, mind looks for a way to secure its survival. It looks for a mate, a friend; it creates the world. But when it begins to get too much—too many connections, too much world—it rejects it; it creates a little niche somewhere or other and fights for that tooth and nail in order to survive. Sometimes mind loses the game. And then mind ceases to be mind. It becomes psychotic, completely mad. You "lose your mind," as we say. You are completely overcrowded by the whole projection of the world. You cannot even function on an ordinary logical level. Such psychosis results from either of the two extremes: overcrowdedness, or, on the other hand, lack of anything for mind to work with. So mind can only exist in the neurosis of relative reference, not in psychosis. When it reaches the psychotic level, mind ceases to function as mind. It becomes something else, something poisonous.

Q: According to that model, how would meditation practice affect the relationship between mind and the world it's in battle with?

R: The purpose of meditation practice is to try to save oneself from the psychosis.

Q: But you still maintain the world? I mean you still maintain the neurotic state, basically?

R: Not necessarily, either. There is another alternative mind which does not need the neurotic world. This is where the idea of enlightenment comes in. Enlightened mind can go further and further, beyond questions of relative reference. It does not have to keep up with this world. It reaches a point where it does not have to sharpen itself on this neurotic world any more. There is another level of experience which still has reference point but in a much clearer way. In this case it is reference point without demand, reference point that does not need further reference point. That is called nonduality. The possibility does exist of developing a higher level of duality which does not involve the dualistic approach as such; and this is called nonduality. This does not mean to say that you dissolve into the world or the world becomes you. It's not a question of oneness but rather a question of zeroness.

Q: Rinpoche, how does the notion of mind that you've talked about relate to the notion of ego and the strategies of maintaining ego?

R: Mind, as we have been talking about it, is ego. Ego can survive only in relation to a reference point, not by itself. But I am trying to make the whole thing quite simple and relate it directly to the practice of meditation. If we think practicing meditation is concerned with working with our ego, that sounds like too big a deal. Whereas if we just work with mind, that is an actual, real thing to us. In order to wake up in the morning you have to know it is morning—there is light outside and you have awakened. Those simple things are a perfect example of basic ego. Ego survives and thrives on reference point. So *sems* is ego, yes.

Q: You talked about the mind relating to externals only. What do you consider it when the mind is functioning in pure intellection or imagination, creating its own object, so to speak.

R: That is external.

Q: But there could be nothing out there. You could be in a darkened cell and be imagining hearing a symphony, for example, and it exists only in your mind.

R: Sure. That is outside. That seems to be the point. Maybe you are not really talking to me now. Maybe you are in a dark room and you are talking to your version of me. Somehow the physical visual situation is not that important a factor. Any mental object, mental content, is regarded as an external thing.

Q: In regard to the technique of breathing, is there any particular reason why we identify with the outbreath rather than the inbreath?

R: That's a question of openness. You have to create some kind of gap, some area where there is less strain. Once you breathe out, you're sure to breathe in again, so there's room for relief of some kind. Nothing needs watching there.

Another thing is that outbreathing is an expression of stepping out of your centralized system. Outbreathing has nothing to do with centralizing in your body, where usually everything is psychosomatically bottled up. Instead, by identifying with the outbreath you are sharing, you are giving something out.

Q: When you were talking about the "flat-bottomed" ideas, you said something like having that flat bottom is what provides an openness or a space, as opposed to having wings on your mind, flying thoughts or whatever. What makes that panic arise that made the retreatant turn to the book and that makes us run away from that sense of groundedness?

R: A lot of fear comes when things are too clearly defined for you. The situation becomes overwhelmingly sharp and direct and accurate, so that you would rather interpret it than simply acknowledge it. It is like when you say something very plain and direct to someone and you find him saying, "In other words, you are saying, blah, blah, blah, blah, blah." Instead of relating directly to what has been said, there is a tendency to try to keep your twist. That seems to be a problem of shyness from the bluntness of reality, being shy of that formness, that thingness that exists in our world that nobody faces. Facing

that is the highest form of sanity and enlightened vision. This seems to be the basic point of certain descriptions in the *Tibetan Book of the Dead*, where it talks about a bright light coming towards you that you shy away from; you are frightened of it. Then there is a dull, seductive light coming from one of the six realms of neurotic existence and you are attracted instead to that. You prefer the shadow to the reality. That is the kind of problem that exists. Often the reality is so blunt and outrageous and overwhelming that you feel facing it would be like sitting on a razorblade.

Q: You have spoken of experiencing the body. There are a lot of techniques, practices for feeling the body, where attention will be focused on the physical sensation or tension or whatever you feel when you attempt to feel the physical body. I'm wondering now what relation that kind of practice would have to the practice with the breath that you described. Are those techniques a different thing or would they reinforce the practice with the breath?

R: Your breath *is* your physical body from the point of view of this approach. There are all kinds of sensations that you experience along with the breath—pains, aches, itches, pleasurable feelings and so on. You experience all those things along with the breath. Breath is the theme and the other things go along with it. So the idea of the breathing technique is simply to be very precise about what you are experiencing. You relate to those sensations as they come up, along with your breath, without imagining that you are experiencing your body. Those experiences are not at all your body's experiences. That is impossible. Actually, you are in no way in a position to experience your body. Those experiences are just thoughts—"I'm thinking I'm in pain." It is the thought of pain, the thought of itch and so forth.

Q: So are you saying that the breathing technique is in a way a saner attitude than believing that "Now I'll feel my body," and making a project out of that?

R: The breathing technique is a literal one, a direct one. It faces what is actually the case rather than just trying to turn out some result.

Q: Before you were saying that when you're sitting here and you're taking notes, or focused on the speaker and relaxing, that's a psychosomatic notion of body. And psychosomatic, the way I understand it, is sort of an imagined thing or something that has to do with your mind, with how your mind is affecting your body. Like a psychosomatic disease—your mind has some effect on your body. How is that related to the fact that you're sitting here relaxing and listening to a speaker? How is that a psychosomatic sense of body?

R: The point is that, whatever we do in our lives, we don't actually just do it, we are affected by mind. Maybe the body, actually the true body, is being pressured by the psychosomatic speed of the mind. You might say that there is a possibility that you might be sitting here now properly, in a non-psychosomatic way. But still the whole situation of sitting here was brought together, the whole incident was moved into place, by psychosomatic driving force. So your sitting here was set up by the psychosomatic system, basically. If you have some kind of psycho-somatic convulsion and you throw up, actually you do throw up stuff, which is not psychosomatic stuff. It is body stuff, but it is manifested in psychosomatic style. Its being thrown up was instigated by psychosomatic process. That is the kind of situation we are in. Fundamentally our whole world is psychosomatic, from that point of view. The whole process of living is composed of psychosomatic hangups. The desire to listen to the teachings comes from beginning to be aware of one's hangups. Since you have begun to be aware of your hangups you would like to create this further hangup to clear up the existing hangups.

Q: Instead of relating directly?

R: Well, one never does that until one has some kind of flashes of something on the level of enlightenment. Until that point everything one does is always by innuendo.

Q: So any kind of disease or anything that's affecting you is psychosomatic?

R: It is not only disease that is psychosomatic. Your process of health is psychosomatic already. Actual disease is sort of an extra thing, like yeast growing on top of your back.

Q: Rinpoche, speaking about "touch and go," if a fantasy arises, to what point do you allow that fantasy to develop before you let go of it?

R: Once it arises, that is already "touch." Then let it be as it is. Then it goes. There is a peak point there. First, there is creation of the fantasy; then it reaches maturity; then it is beyond its prime; and then it slowly vanishes or tries to turn into something else.

Q: Sometimes a fantasy will turn into a whole emotional plot which seems to get more and more complex.

R: That is beating a dead horse. You just let it come, play out its impetus or energy, then just let go. You have to taste it, then let it go. Having tasted it, it is not recommended to manipulate it any further.

Q: When you speak of "touch and go," evidently meditating, sitting practice, is the "touch." Do you mean also there are times when it's inappropriate to be mindful in this manner? That in everyday life we should just let mindfulness go?

R: I think there is some misunderstanding there. "Touch" and "go" always come together. It is like whenever there is a one there is a zero. The number series, starting with one, implies zero. Numbers do not make sense if there is no such thing as zero. "Touch" has no meaning without "go." They are simultaneous. That simultaneity is mindfulness, which happens both during formal sitting practice and the postmeditation experience of everyday life.

Q: Previously, you mentioned the retreatant who had the feeling of sitting on a razorblade when things became very clear, very distinct. Could you relate that experience to the sense of delight in the mindfulness of livelihood?

R: It is the same experience, actually. Whenever there is a threat of death, that also brings a sense of life. It is like taking a pill because if you don't take it you might die. That pill is associated with the threat of death, but you take it with the attitude that it will enable you to live. Facing the moment clearly is like taking that pill. It is the fear of death and love of life simultaneously.

Q: How does mindfulness of life inform ethical behavior, ethical action?

R: Things are done without mindfulness in the samsaric world; we thrive on that. Consequently, almost everything we do is somewhat disjointed; somehow it doesn't click, it doesn't fit. There is something illogical about our whole approach. We might be very reasonable, good people; still, behind the facade we are somewhat off. There is fundamental neurosis taking place all the time on our part, which in turn creates pain for other people as well as ourselves. People get hurt by that and their reactions create more of the same. That is what we call the neurotic world or samsara. Nobody is actually having a good time. Even ostensibly good times are somewhat pushed. And the undercurrent of frustration from sensing that creates further indulgence.

Mindfulness of livelihood is an entirely different approach, in which life is treated as precious, which is to say, in some sense, mindfully. Things are seen in their own right rather than as aspects of the vicious cycle of neurosis. Everything is jointed rather than disjointed. One's state of mind becomes coherent so there is a basic workability concerning how, in a general sense, to conduct one's life. One begins to become literate in reading the style of the world, the pattern of the world. That is the starting point, by no means the final stage. It is just beginning to see how to read the world.

Q: I really cannot imagine what experience would be like without all kinds of imagination and projections. I can't get a sense of participation in the world just as it is, just as things are occurring and coming up.

R: Well, are you interested in finding that out?

Q: I guess so.

R: Well, it is very hard to do. The reason it is hard is that you are doing it. It is like looking for a lost horse. In order to look for it, you need to ride your lost horse. On the other hand, maybe you are riding on your lost horse, but still you are looking for it. It is something like that. It's one of those.

You see, there is really no such thing as ultimate reality. If there was such a thing, for that reason alone that could not be it. That is the problem. So you are back to square one. And the only thing, it seems that you can do is practice. That is good enough.

Q: In connection with the flash of waking up in the mindfulness of effort, I still don't clearly understand where you are supposed to come back from and what you are supposed to come back to.

R: Once the flash happens, you do not have to find out where you came from and appreciate it. That is what I mean about not entertaining the messenger. You also do not need an idea of where you are going. After the flash, your awareness is like a snowflake released from the clouds. It is going to settle down to the ground anyhow. You have no choice.

Q: Sometimes being mindful of the exhalation seems to become too deliberate. It seems too much that the watcher is doing it from above, rather than the breathing and the mindfulness being simultaneous.

R: The touch-and-go approach is applicable here. You touch the exhalation and then disown the awareness even of that. If you are trying to have bare attention constantly, then you have a problem of being very rigid and dragging yourself along. So you touch with the breath and go with the breath. That way there is a sense of freshness, a change of air. It is like a pulsation; or like listening to a musical beat. While you are trying to keep with one beat, you miss another. But that way you begin to hear the rhythm; and then you hear the entirety of the music, too. It is the same way with any experience. Another example is eating food. When we eat food, we don't taste it constantly, just now and then. We hover around our interest. Always we just touch the highlights of our interest. So the touch-and-go style of mindfulness practice is borrowed from the basic style of mind. If you go along with that, then there is no problem at all.

Q: I somewhat understand how mindfulness of mind is a one-shot movement. But then if effort comes in, that no longer seems simultaneous or spontaneous.

R: Effort comes in off and on, at the beginning, during and at the end. For instance, you are holding that microphone because you had an interest in asking a question. Now while you are listening to the answer, you have forgotten that you are holding the microphone, but that original effort is still hanging over. You are still holding it, not dropping it. So a lot of journeys back and forth take place with one's effort, rather than its being maintained constantly. Therefore you do not have to strain and push constantly. If you do, there is no practice, no meditation. The whole thing just becomes a big deal of effort. That shifting, alternating constantly, creates the space of meditation. If you are one hundred percent effortful, you blow the whole thing. There is nothing left but a tense lump of muscle sitting in the middle of a field. This happens all the time in life situations. It is like trying to knead dough. If you knead too hard you don't have any dough left in your hand, you are just pushing your hand against the board. You can knead dough hard if you have the feeling that the purpose of kneading hard is to work with the dough. Then you have some compromises taking place, some intelligence comes into play. Without that, effort alone just kills.

Q: Without exercising some kind of incredible deliberateness, my entire meditation practice seems to be fantasy. There seems to be hardly any time of relating with my breath. It is basically just sitting there daydreaming or else very deliberately, heavyhandedly trying to relate with my breath.

R: Well, go and sit.

Q: What should I do when I sit?

R: Sit.

Q: That's all? What about working with my breath?

R: Sit. Go ahead and sit. Just go ahead and do it.

THE PREPARATORY STAGE

People in all ages have been under stress and have devised and tried various means to escape from it, only to find to their dismay that the stress did not disappear but reasserted itself in other forms as threatening as before, if not even worse. This shows that escape is never an answer to the basic question of how to be a human being. Escape, whether it is into the mechanical uniformity and monotony of social conformity or into a fictitious world of some transcendental make-believe, is but an admission of having failed in the everpresent task of growing up. The latter form of escape is particularly dangerous as it leads a person to believe that he has enlarged his scope of awareness, while actually he has run away from it; and instead of having gained insight, he has blurred his view and diminished his capacity for thought by clinging to such fetish words as science, or creativity or even intelligence. The attempted escape from stress has brought no vision which alone would have provided a basis for dealing with the problem at hand. Vision brings a new appreciation of what there is, it makes a person see things differently, rather than see different things. After all nobody can ever escape Being, least of all his own being. It is the vision that gives meaning to our experiences and our actions by making us face the problem, and therefore also vision alone gives man a sense of direction and enables him to sketch a map which will guide him in his task of finding himself rather than running away from himself.

However, vision does not come on demand; it requires for its birth sustained intellectual effort which is, above all, the act of being appreciative and, for that reason also, discriminative; it also demands unflagging diligence and a firm foundation on which the unificatory processes leading to an integrated personality can rest. There is a gradation in this preliminary build-up, one step leading to the other; hence the attempt to make light or even to skip the preliminaries, because modern man is in a hurry and must have instant results, is as intelligent or stupid as trying to prepare a succulent meal without having the necessary ingredients.

It is for this reason that the preparatory stage of the Buddhist "path"[1] has been given considerable attention in indigenous works,

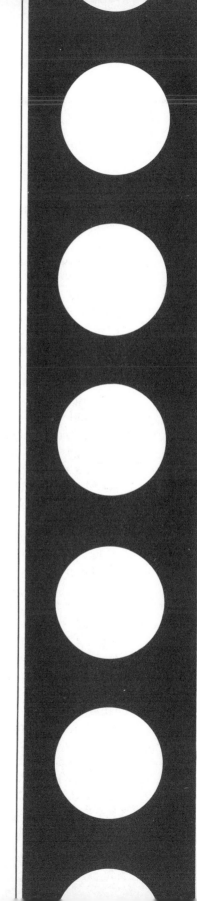

while it has been more or less neglected by those who have approached Buddhist ideas from outside. The preparatory stage is graded into three sections which present a gradation and intensification of awareness. The first section begins with four kinds of inspection. Inspection, in the strict sense of the word, is the attempt to keep a perceptual situation as constant as possible and to inspect the objective constituent of that perceptual situation as closely as possible. However, keeping a perceptual situation constant is intimately intertwined with the attempt to learn more about the qualities of the perceived object—the objective constituent and the epistemological object of the perceptual situation. Thus we may say that, on the one hand, we keep an idea or an image or an "object" of the mind constant and, on the other, we apply the appreciative and discriminative capacity of the mind to the idea or image or object held as constant as possible. In other words, "inspection" presupposes appreciative discrimination just as "appreciative discrimination" presupposes inspection.

The objective constituent of an inspective situation is said to be what, for all practical purposes, we may call "the body." With it we associate the notion of "physical object" and this widens the range of what is meant by "body" in Buddhist texts. It comprises everything that is subsumed under the term *rupa-skandha* (*gzugs-kyi phung-po*) which may be rendered freely as "everything that has color-form." More precisely, the term rupa indicates an epistemological object of a perceptual situation which we would further characterize as "of the physical kind." This does not say anything about whether there is or is not an ontological object corresponding to the epistemological one. In this wider sense "body" is now classified as "external," "internal," and "intermediate." These three specifications refer to what we are wont to call "objective," "subjective" and "ambiguous." There is no difficulty about the connotations of "subjective." It is our body—my body—as the capacity for feeling and thinking. "Objective" does not refer to another's body, as might be concluded from the use of the term "body," but it refers to the physical environment which is constituted by the interaction of elemental forces. "Ambiguous" ("intermediate") is another's body. It is "ambiguous" because the other is at once subject and object—he is subject and as such is and has his own body, while he is object for me, being and having my body. This distinction between three kinds of "body" is important as it has distinct consequences for man's dealings with others and, implicitly, himself.

In the same way as the "body" may be the objective constituent of an inspective situation, so also a feeling may be something about which I want to learn more. Inasmuch as feelings are pleasant, unpleasant or neutral, their qualification in this manner are, more precisely, inspective judgments based on the inspection of the objective constituent which is both an objective and nonreferential mental event.

This leads to the inspection of "mind" which is a complex of a specific kind, not an isolated event. It is this complex that becomes the objective mental situation which I then know directly.

Lastly, there are the "meanings" which are defined by concepts and motivations. What something *means* for somebody depends upon what he is doing or is planning to do. A person, in a situation described as "seeing a red light," treats his visual sensum as the appearance of a physical object and acts as if there is a causal connection between the color red and danger. At a later stage he may even make reflective judgments about these "meanings."

It is one thing to know how to pinpoint the objective constituents of inspective situations, it is another to know what to learn from them. It is here that the difference between hinayana and mahayana becomes most marked:

> The follower of the hinayana deals with the "body" as impure, with "feeling" as unpleasant, with "mind" as impermanent and with "meanings" as having no ontological status; the follower of the mahayana deals with these four topics, when in a state of composure, as if they were like the sky beyond all propositions about them and, in a post-composure state, as if they were an apparition or a dream.[2]

The traditional Buddhist axioms of the impermanence, unpleasantness (frustration) and essencelessness of all that we normally encounter are readily recognizable and need no further elaboration. Impurity, however, presents a problem as it may easily lead to a disassociation of the personality by overevaluating one aspect of man's Being and denigrating another; above all it creates an opposition between ideas or postulates and experiences. To see the body as impure may consolidate into a rejection of the body, and since its "impure" image is an abstraction that becomes superimposed on the living body, a person cannot but feel frustrated and will attempt to escape into a "purer" realm which is no less an abstraction. This, of course, is an extreme case, but it also reveals an intellectualistic and basically egocentered approach to Being. When the body is pictured as a rotting corpse, it becomes an object of disgust and easily engenders a host of negative emotions which eventually will blot out the value of being, even of being human. The same holds good for feelings, as well as for the other topics of inspection.

However it would be wrong to conceive of the insistence on the impurity of the body merely in this negative way. Inasmuch as the hinayana also aims at man's health and at an integrated personality, the idea of impurity may have some therapeutic effect in releasing the person from his bondage to the physical side of his being and in enabling him to discover the deep intrinsic values he is pursuing. But because of his egocenteredness these values are much more difficult to find. The ego is steeped in images and roles and averse to experience, if not afraid of it. Even if we admit that it is an experience that prompted us to label our body as impure or our feelings as frustrating, in so classifying the experience we have cut ourselves off from the possibility of seeing our being with complete freshness. There again the difference between hinayana and mahayana becomes evident. The former is preoccupied with judgments of perception and its abstractions, the latter starts from and attempts to maintain vividness of experience:

The followers of the hinayana take as their objective reference merely the four topics of inspection as they relate to themselves and others. The concrete form they give to the pursuance of these ideas is that the followers of the hinayana contemplate them in terms of impurity and so on, while the followers of the mahayana contemplate them in their openness of being. The aim they have is that the followers of the hinayana contemplate these topics in order to become detached from the disturbingly frail and fragile body and so on, while the followers of the mahayana do not contemplate them for the sake of being or not being detached from it, but for the sake of realizing a nirvana that is in no way fixated.[3]

Thus, in one case, a person remains within the limits of a dichotomous way of thinking which implies something "higher" as contrasted with something "lower" that is spurned and repudiated; while, in the other, the person is capable of an integrative way of thinking which does not imply a cutting off of the "outer" world so as to permit the "inner" world to come into play, but lives the inner and outer simultaneously.

Inspection as a means to learn more about a given situation is indispensable for any progress on the path. By virtue of being the capacity to hold a situation as constant as possible, it also leads to concentration, which is one of the phenomena of the second phase in the preparatory stage. This second phase is known as the "four abandonings" which actually is a summary term for the elimination of negative factors as well as the intensification of positive factors, both processes going hand in hand. Thus by "elimination" the intention not to allow negative factors to arise and the intention to put an end to their presence is understood, while "intensification" is allowing the positive factors to come into operation and to develop and intensify their presence.

At the beginning of this phase stands "interest," which is followed by four other processes. "Interest" is, as it were, a first stirring of a self-awakening by which we are given the chance to get out of the normal attitude of apathy and inner emptiness so characteristic of the prevailing mood of boredom. All of a sudden, so it seems, "interest" lets us look at life more keenly; and this involves a willingness to differentiate, which is rooted in a conviction that gives man a sense of purpose and meaning. Thus "'interest' comes by one's faith in one's ability to differentiate, that is, to accept and to reject."[4]

ཀྱི་བོ། །ཁ་ལག་དང་པོ་དེས་འདགའ་ཝག་ལ་ལན་འགྱུར་བ་ཆེ་བ་དེ་དགའི་གི་བསྐུབ་པ་ལ་རྗེས་སུ་སློ་བ་ཡི། །རྗེས་སུ་བསྐུབ་ཡི། །ལ་ཕར་ག་ཡེམ་པ་དང་། །བདུང་དུ་སྐུབ་པ་དང་། །འབུ་ཆིན་དང་བ་ཉིས་པ་ཆེན་སྐུས་པ་ར་འབྱུར་བ་བཝག་ནེ་པ་འི་གནས་སུ་ཆག །འདིས་ན་བཟུང་སྟེ། །རྗེས་འཆིན་རདུམ་བྱེ་པ་ལེ་ནས་པ་དང་། །འདང་བ་ལ་ཕོག་གར་ག་ཡེམ་པ་དང་། །བདུང་དུ་སྐུབ་ཡི་བའི་གནས་ལས་སུ་སྐྱོ་ཝིག་ལ་པ་ར་འབྱུར་བོ། །ཁ་ལག་ལུ་པ་དེས་འདང་དགའ་ཝག་ལས་པ་ད་ག་བཙམ་པ་དེ་དགའི་གི་བསྐུབ་པ་ལ་རྗེ་དབ་ར་འབྱུར། །རྒོ་བསྐྱེ་ནེ་དེ་དགྱེ་བར་ སྐུབ་པའི་ཚིག་རྟོགས་སོ།། །དེ་འི་ག་དུ་གང་ག་ཡ་ས་དེ་ཞུ་བར་ཉེད་འི་ དབ་ར་ནེ་འགའ་ལ་ཚོ་ས་ཆ་དུ་ར་འགྱུར་རོ། །དེ་འི་ཡོག་ཏུན་འ་དེ་བོ་སྟོང་ གི་ས་ཙུབ་ར་བྱུའི། །འ་ཌི་ལུ་སྟུབ་ཡ་དུ་སྐ། གནས་ བྱུ་བར་འགྱུར་པ་ལ་འང་དུ་སྟ། །གནས་འང་བོ་སོ་ན་བོང་བ་པ་ལ་འ་ར་དུ་སྟེ། །ནི་རྔ་མས་ལ་ ཕུ་ག་འ་ཚལ་དུ་བཙུ་ག་ན་ས་ཚོ་ག

Interest is certainly shortlived if it is not followed by efforts to affirm a way of acting as part of our vision of reality which is our life's meaning. Such an effort is a decision. It implies that an action has been chosen and that the person will stay with his decision. Again, "'decision' is not to let the mind [go] elsewhere."[5]

Any decision involves a risk. Things may go well and we may be lured into a false sense of elation or they may go wrong and we may be swallowed up by a mood of depression. Not to succumb to these mood swings needs "sustained effort." More precisely, "sustained effort" serves to strike a balance, to build a firm ground on which a person can proceed. Elation takes a person off the ground, it makes him overexcited and produces an ego inflation. But every feeling of elation is bound to collapse and a depressive reaction will ensue. Depression makes a person fall emotionally into an abysmal hole. Thus, "'sustained effort' serves to calm such occurrences as elation and depression."[6] Since there is sustained effort, "to calm" does not mean to make a person passive and without feelings. Rather, it makes him strong so that when that which might turn into feelings of elation or moods of depression is about to occur, he can cope with the situation.

This coping with the situation takes two different lines of action. One is to pull the mind back from becoming immobilized and engulfed in utter gloom and to direct it towards man's existential reality which is his inner potential, not a fantasy world of unreal goals. The other is to confront the mind with the harsh and indisputable facts of the world in which we live. This is another way of bringing a person back and putting him on solid ground. Man's existential reality is the quality and meaning life has for him. This comes to him in symbolic form as the Buddha personage, infinitely rich in qualities, which is the beacon light guiding and directing the traveller on his journey to his inner strength. As such it is heartening and comforting and energizing; it can give what the depressed person is in need of: "Taking a firm grip on mind is to direct it towards something which makes it feel happy, such as the Buddha personage and his qualities, when it has slipped into the gloominess of depression."[7]

Similarly, it is as important to keep the mind in touch with reality, to "bring it down" when it is flying off into the illusion that everything will work out splendidly, that things could never be better: "Bringing the mind down is to direct it towards something that is distasteful such as the frustration of samsara, when it has taken off into overexcitement and elation."[8]

The second phase of this preparatory stage is therefore what we would call a kind of balancing which, precisely because here the individual is not torn one way or another, offers the chance for a wider perspective. This is opened up in particular in the third phase which involves supernormal perceptions and wholeness experiences. Supernormal perceptions include such phenomena as multiple personality, which is more easily understandable in view of the Buddhist concept of mind as a structure rather than as a single particle. A structure can well be multidimensional and be something that has size and shape by analogy, and it also can intersect with other similar structures. Another phenomenon on this level is the "knowledge of other minds." The argument for it is by analogy. It assumed that "there is another mind animating a body as my mind is animating my body."[9] There certainly are experiences about which we believe that there are in them certain mental states which are not ours but belong to other minds. Although we ordinarily proceed without questioning or being aware of this assumption, it is here raised to a conscious affirmation which enables us to deal with others as "subjects" rather than as objects.

Another phenomenon is the activation of mnemic persistents. As has been pointed out, "mind" in Buddhist psychology is a complex that, among other structural elements, includes a factor that is capable of carrying modifications of experiences which happen to a person during his life. If such a "psychic factor" unites with a new body or enters into an intimate relationship with a new situation, it will not be surprising that there are "memories" of a previous life. In no way does this necessitate the assumption of an "eternal" principle such as a self or pure ego.

While such supernormal phenomena as these may occur, they are not of paramount importance. Rather emphasis is to be put upon wholeness experiences, of which four are most significant for the development of the personality. In each of them a specific operation takes place and each of them constitutes a "foothold" for the above phenomena and their experience. They are interest, sustained effort, focusedness and scrutiny. These operations essentially serve to preserve the wholeness experiences by counteracting whatever threatens to disrupt them. Thus, we are told, there are five disruptive forces and these are encountered by eight "eliminating operations." The following diagram shows their interaction:

FIVE DISRUPTIVE FORCES	EIGHT ELIMINATING OPERATIONS
	serious interest
	inner conviction
laziness	sustained effort
	cultivation of the inner potential
forgetfulness (letting the object of one's concern slip from one's mind)	inspection

depression and elation	alert awareness
not doing anything about either state	intent and focusing
overdoing things when either state has subsided	equanimity

The three phases of the preparatory stage, each having a specific set of operations, deal only with what is necessary for setting out on one's lifelong quest for meaning. Though this is merely the preparatory stage of the path, it already demands the utmost of us. Yet, since it is only a first step in the direction of self-growth, it does not guarantee that we will succeed in our quest. Only the barest ingredients are presented, now it depends upon us what we do with them. It is as if we have collected all that is necessary for a delicious meal; still we have to make the meal ready and in doing this we can still spoil everything. The complexity of the preparatory stage and all that is involved in it leaves no room for transcendental mystification and the effort that is needed is the opposite of that needed to follow any cheap commercial recipe.

NOTES

1 The "path" as a whole comprises five stages: a preparatory one; a stage of application which links all that has been done and experienced with the third stage—the "path of seeing." This in turn merges into the "path of cultivation," which is to live one's life in the light of the vision; and, finally, the "stage of no-more-learning," which means that we cannot act except as fully integrated personalities.

2 *bDen-gnyis gsal-byed zla-ba'i sgron-ma*, a detailed commentary on Kun-mkhyen 'Jigs med-gling-pa's *Yon-tan-mdzod*, by mKhan-po Yon-dga'. Vol. I p. 274.
mKhan-po Yon-dga' seems to have been a contemporary of gZhan-dga' (1871-1927). He derives much of his information from the works of Klong-chen-rab-'byams-pa (1308-1363), the foremost rNying-ma-pa sage.

3 *ibid.*, p. 274.

4 *ibid.*, p. 275.

5 *ibid.*

6 *ibid.*

7 *ibid.*

8 *ibid.*

9 *ibid.*, p. 276.

10 For further details see H. V. Guenther and L. S. Kawamura, *Mind in Buddhist Psychology*, Dharma Publishing 1975, pp. 118f.

Song of the White Banner

Last night I dreamt my only father guru, Padma Trime, was carrying a white banner with a blue HUM that fluttered in the wind. He was riding on a white horse without harness. The horse trotted on the surface of the ocean. As I awoke, the bittersweet memory inspired this song.

Father incomparable, lord guru,
When you are riding the white horse of dharmata,
You are not shaken by the waves of conditioned truth;
In the unchanging simplicity of insight,
You fly the banner of self-existing HUM.

As you travel in the space of joy and emptiness,
Your actions are like those of a white garuda;
You are not shaken by dualistic views,
Whatever you see is the dance of dharmakaya.

When you reside in the castle of the practicing lineage,
Your actions are those of Vajradhara,
You are singing the songs of mahamudra,
The three worlds are filled with lineage holders.

When you are in the highlands of fearlessness,
Your actions are like those of a high snow-mountain,
The sleet of wisdom is all-pervasive,
You court the compassion of the white clouds.

When you are roaming in the jungle of samsara,
Your actions are like those of a tiger,
You cut the head of the beast of ego,
You consume the innards of hope and fear.

When remembering the father's actions,
His son wakes from a dream into joy and emptiness;
How delightful to enjoy the feast of mahamudra.
May this song of one taste liberate the threefold world.

December 28, 1974

The Basic Ground
and the Eight Consciousnesses

We could begin by discussing the origin of all psychological problems, neurotic mind. Neurotic mind is a tendency to identify oneself with desires and conflicts related to a world outside. Accomplishing this projection immediately creates an uncertainty as to whether such conflicts actually exist externally or whether they are internal, whether they are really real or one is making them up. This uncertainty solidifies the whole sense that a problem of some kind exists; and this sense of problem is the working basis for ego. What is real? What is not real? That is always our biggest problem. It is ego's problem.

The abhidharma, which comprises the basic Buddhist teachings on psychology, is based on the point of view of egolessness. Egolessness does not mean simply the absence of ego itself. It means also the absence of the projections of ego. Egolessness comes more or less as a by-product of seeing the transitory, transparent nature of the world outside. Once we have dealt with the projections of ego and seen their transitory and transparent nature, then ego has no reference point. So the notions of inside and outside are interdependent—ego began and its projections began. Ego manages to maintain its identity by means of its projections. When we are able to see the projections as nonsubstantial, ego becomes transparent correspondingly.

According to the abhidharma, ego consists, in one of its aspects, of eight kinds of consciousness. There are the six sense consciousnesses (the aspect of mind that coordinates the sense world is regarded as a sixth sense). Then there is a seventh consciousness, which has the nature of ignorance, cloudiness, confusion. This cloudy mind is an overall structure which runs right through the six sense consciousnesses. It is blind, an absence of precision. Each sense consciousness relates to this cloudy situation of not knowing exactly what one is doing.

The eighth consciousness is what could be called the common ground or the unconscious ground of all this. It is the ground that makes it possible for all the other seven to operate. This ground is different from the fundamental basic ground which is the background of all of existence and contains samsara and nirvana both. The eighth consciousness is not as basic as that ground. It is a kind of secondary basic level where confusion has already begun; and that confusion provides an accommodation for the other seven consciousnesses to operate.

There is an evolutionary process which starts from the unconscious ground, the eighth consciousness. The cloudy consciousness arises from that and then the six sense consciousnesses. Even the six senses evolve in a certain order according to the level of experiential intensity of each of them. The most intense level is attained with sight, which develops last.

These eight types of consciousness can be looked at as being on the level of the first of the five skandhas, form. They are the form of ego, the tangible aspect of it. They constitute the ultimate grounding element of ego—as far as ego's grounding goes, which is not very far. Still, from a relative point of view, they do comprise something fixed, something definite.

I think, to place this in perspective, it would be good to discuss briefly—even though the abhidharma teaching does not talk very much about it—the fundamental basic ground, the all-pervading basic ground which we have just contrasted to the eighth consciousness. This basic ground does not depend on relative situations at all. It is natural being which just is. Energies appear out of this basic ground and those energies are the source of the development of relative situations. Sparks of duality, intensity and sharpness, flashes of wisdom and knowledge—all sorts of things come out of the basic ground. So the basic ground is the source of confusion and also the source of liberation. Both liberation and confusion are that energy which happens constantly, which sparks out and then goes back to its basic nature, like clouds (as Milarepa described it) emerging from and disappearing back into the sky.

As for ego's type of ground, the eighth consciousness, this arises when the energy which flashes out of the basic ground brings about a sort of blinding effect, bewilderment. That bewilderment becomes the eighth consciousness, the basic ground for ego. Dr. Guenther calls it "bewilderment-errancy." It is error that comes out of being bewildered—a kind of panic. If the energy were to go along with its own process of speed, there would be no panic. It is like driving a car fast; if you go along with the speed, you are able to maneuver accordingly. But if you suddenly panic with the thought that you have been going too fast without realizing it, you jam on the brakes and probably have an accident. Something suddenly freezes and brings the bewilderment of not knowing how to conduct the situation. Then actually the situation takes you over. Rather than remaining completely one with the projection, the projection takes you over. The unexpected power of the projection comes back to you as your own doing, which creates extremely powerful and impressive bewilderment. That bewilderment acts as the basic ground, the secondary basic ground of ego, away from the primordial basic ground.

So ego is the ultimate relative, the source of all the relative concepts in the whole samsaric world. You cannot have criteria, notions of comparison, relationships of this and that, without ego. Things begin from ego's impression of relativity. Even nirvana begins that way. When ego began, nirvana, the other side of the same coin, began also. Without ego, there could be no such thing as nirvana or liberation, since a free state without relativity would already be the case. So as ego develops, freedom and imprisonment begin to exist; and that relative situation contains the basic quality of ignorance.

The abhidharma does not talk very much about ignorance in the fundamental sense of ignoring oneself, but understanding this will add a further dimension to the teaching of the eight consciousnesses. Once there is bewilderment, a sort of double take begins to happen of then wanting to find out where you were and what you are. But the nature of the bewilderment is that you do not really want to go back and find out your original situation. Instead you want to get your bearings in terms of the frame of reference bewilderment has created. Since, with the bewilderment, you have created something to latch onto, you want to ignore the case history that led to that altogether. You want to make the best of that present bewilderment and cling to it. That is the ignoring—refusing to go back because it is too painful, too frightening. As they say, "ignorance is bliss." Ignoring of ignoring is bliss, at least from ego's point of view.

This understanding of ignorance comes from the mahamudra teaching of the vajrayana tradition. The difference between the abhidharma and basic sutra teachings on ignorance and the more direct and daring mahamudra teaching is that the sutra and abhidharma teaching relates to ignorance as a one-way process—bewilderment and grasping and the six sense consciousnesses develop and ignorance takes over. Then ignorance is viewed as a solid thing that has to be combated. But in the vajrayana teaching, ignorance is seen not only from the angle of the development of ego, but also as containing the potential for wisdom. This is not mentioned at all in the lower teachings. But within the eight consciousnesses, including the six sense consciousnesses, there actually is the possibility of ignorance turning into wisdom. This is a key point because wisdom cannot be born from theory; it must be born from your actual existing state of mind, which is the working basis for all spiritual practice.

The wisdom of dealing with situations as they are, and that is what wisdom is, contains tremendous precision that could not come from anywhere else but the physical situations of sight, smell, feeling, touchable objects and sounds. The earthy situation of actual things as they are is the source of wisdom. You can become completely one with smell, with sight, with sound, and your knowledge *about* them ceases to exist; your knowledge becomes wisdom. There is nothing to know about things as an external educational process. You become completely one with them: complete relationship takes place with sounds, smells, sights and so on. This approach is at the core of the mandala principle of the vajrayana teaching. At the same time, the great importance given to the six sense consciousnesses in the abhidharma has a similar concrete significance in its application to the practice of meditation and a person's way of relating to his experiences. Both levels of teaching put tremendous emphasis on direct relationship with the down-to-earth aspect of experience.

Questions and Answers

Question: Can you say more about how the six senses connect up with meditation?

Rinpoche: The implication of the abhidharma teaching on the six senses for the practice of meditation is identifying yourself with sounds, touchable objects, feelings, breathing and so on. The only way to develop sound meditative technique is to take something ordinary and use that. Unless you take something simple, the whole state of mind of your meditation will be based on the conflict of what is real and what is not and your relationship to that. This brings all kinds of complications and one begins to interpret these complications as psychological problems, neurotic problems, and to develop a sort of paranoid frame of mind in which what is going on represents to one much more than is actually there. So the whole idea is to start by relating to nonduality on a practical level, to step out of these paranoid conflicts of who in us is controlling who. We should just get into actuality, sights and sounds as they are. A basic part of the tradition of meditation is using the sense perceptions as a way of relating with the earth. They are sort of middlemen for dealing with the earth. They contain neither good nor bad, are connected with neither spirituality nor samsara, nor anything at all. They are just neutral.

Q: Ignorance seems to take on different values at different times, if I understand you. Could you explain that further?

R: Ignorance is an evolutionary process. It does not just happen as one lump result, but develops and grows like a plant. You have a seed and earth and manure; then a plant grows and finally blossoms. As we have said, the beginning of that ignorance is bewilderment, panic. It is the ultimate panic, which does not even contain fear. Being just pure panic, it transcends fear. It is something very meditative in that sense, almost spiritual—a spiritual absorption. It is that profound; it comes right from the depths of your very being. That ignorance is the seed of what you are. It is fundamental, neutral, without any concepts or ideas of any kind. Just pure panic, one hundred percent panic. From this, the cloudiness of the eight consciousnesses develops as an aftereffect. It is like when you get hit and then you get dizzy afterwards.

Q: When you speak of "things as they are," do you mean completely without projections? It is at least theoretically possible to experience things without projections, isn't it? The reason I ask is because if there is an overwhelming quality to experiencing things as they are, then that sense of overwhelmingness would be a projection, wouldn't it?

R: It is definitely possible to experience things without projections. But just things as they are would not be overwhelming. That is dualistic. There would be no quality of over-whelming because overwhelming means "who has got control over who." So the question of overwhelmingness does not arise at all. Seeing things as they are is very, very plain. Because it is so plain, it is colorful and precise. There is no game involved, therefore it is more precise, clearer. It does not need any relative supports; it does not call for any comparisons. That is why the individuality of things is then seen more precisely—because there is no need to compare anything to anything. You see the merit of each situation in its own right, as it is.

Q: With regard to the eight consciousnesses—does it make sense to try to have a direct experience of any one of them isolated from the rest, or is this too abstract a way of going about it?

R: I think that is too abstract. You cannot deal with them purely individually. It is like looking at a person: if you look at a person from the point of view of how fat or how thin he or she is, you still cannot fail to see also that person's head and toes and what clothes he or she is wearing. So in looking at experience from one perspective you see the rest as well. Once we experience one sense consciousness, then what gives that particular sense con-sciousness the quality of consciousness relates it to the others. Each sense consciousness, to a certain extent, contains the overall picture. It must be what it is in relation to some background; it must breathe some air to survive. It is like seeing a flower growing—when you see the flower, you also see the background it is growing out of.

Q: Is everything we experience within the basic ignorance, within the eighth consciousness, including wisdom or higher states of meditation?

R: Yes. That is precisely why it is worthwhile looking into our state of mind.

Q: So then higher states of meditation don't blank out the six senses, for example?

R: Not at all. Of course not. In fact the six sense consciousnesses are heightened. If we regard meditation as just getting into a fog so that you do not see, you do not feel, something is terribly wrong. In that case meditation would reduce one to a zombie. The enlightened man would have to be rescued. Someone would have to feed him and take him to the bathroom. We would have to have an enlightenment ward.

Q: Rinpoche, you spoke of ignorance as not being willing to go back. What is the way back; is it meditation?

R: One is not willing to trace back how one came to be ignorant. But actually one cannot go back literally. One does not really have to go back. Rather one discovers what one was by going more deeply into the present situation. That is the difference between an intuitive approach and an intellectual one. You can go back intellectually, but that does not help; you remain stuck in the same point of view. The whole idea is that if you are able to realize what you are at the present moment without clinging to bewilderment, that is going back. What you are at this moment contains the whole message of what you were. That is really the practice of nonduality in meditation—seeing your present situation and going with it, identifying with the particular sense experiences of sight, smell and so on. Just experience the simplicity of them.

The Psychology of Meditation

Meditation is a way of working with neurosis of ego, so in order to understand the psychology of meditation we must understand the dynamics of that neurosis. According to Buddhist psychology, the basis of ego is the tendency to solidify energy into a barrier that separates space into two entities, "I" and "Other," the space in here and the space out there. This process is technically termed "dualistic fixation." First there is the initial creation of the barrier, which is the sensing of other, and then the inference of inner or I. This is the birth of ego. We identify with what is in here and struggle to relate to what is out there. The barrier causes an imbalance between inside and outside. The struggle to redress the imbalance further solidifies the wall. The irony of the barrier-creating process is that we lose track of the fact that we have created the barrier and, instead, act as if it was always there.

After the initial creation of I and Other, I feels the territory outside itself, determining if it is threatening, attractive or uninteresting. Feeling the environment is followed by impulsive action—passion, aggression, or ignoring—pulling in what is seductive, pushing away what is threatening or repelling, ignoring what is uninteresting or irritating. But feeling and impulsive action are crude ways of defending and enhancing ego. The next response is conceptual discrimination, fitting phenomena into categories, which makes the world much more manageable and intelligible. Finally, whole fantasy worlds are created to shield and entertain ego. Emotions are the highlights of the fantasies while discursive thoughts, images and memories sustain the story line. A story of ego's hopes and fears, victories and defeats, virtues and vices is developed. In highly neurotic people, elaborate subplots or "problems" then develop from the initial drama. The subplots become very complicated and compelling, often overshadowing the main drama. In psychotic people, the subplots completely overshadow the main drama. The different stages of ego development—the initial split of I and Other, feeling, impulse, conceptualization and the various fantasy worlds—are technically referred to in the Buddhist tradition as the five skandhas. From moment to moment the five skandhas are recreated in such a manner that it seems the ego drama is continuous. Clinging to the apparent continuity and solidity of ego, ceaselessly trying to maintain I and Mine, is the root of neurosis. (This effort clashes with the inevitability of change, with the ever-recurring death and birth of ego, and therefore causes suffering.)

One sees the world in terms of I and the Threat, I and the Seduction; and consequently either moves out and tries to grab hold of phenomena or holds back from them, withdrawing into a defensive posture. Such clinging creates a sense of alienation which panics us into struggling to restore the balance that has been upset. Seemingly pleasurable objects become more seductive and, seemingly hostile objects become more threatening. So the more one struggles either to gain pleasure or avoid pain, the more one creates dissatisfaction. One can go so far as to lose contact with the ground, which is psychosis. Or one can stabilize in a defensive way, which is what a neurotic person does.

The particular neurosis you create depends on your style of relating to the world—defensive, seductive, manipulative, encompassing or ignoring. But whatever your style, the degree to which you are neurotic depends on the extent to which you are struggling to make yourself comfortable; which is ironic, because it is the effort to make ourselves comfortable that creates the discomfort.

On the other hand, there is the possibility of breaking the chain of panic and struggle by opening to what is, by dropping the attempt continually to maintain one's security. One can define meditation as a process of letting go, of giving up conflict, not in a passive, spineless sense, but in the sense of being present yet not manipulative. So we are faced with the moment-to-moment alternative of either opening to space, of being in harmony with it, or of solidifying and fixating it.

One must be careful not to fall into the trap of superficially letting go. What one is doing in that case is trying to compensate for the discomfort of life by smoothing it over, by trying to make oneself at ease. In the case of highly neurotic persons, their awkward attempts at easing their discomfort are obvious. But in the case of spiritual techniques such covering over is harder to detect. Rather than softening reality, meditation is a process of clearly seeing it. A good example is Don Juan's approach to fear. He does not offer Carlos a technique to dilute fear. Instead he tells Carlos to live with fear, live with death, make death his companion, make fear his companion; but never succumb to them.

Meditation is thus concerned with life as it is rather than as we would like it to be. From the Buddhist perspective, the realities of life can be summarized in terms of three basic principles—impermanence, suffering and egolessness. The first reality is death—the nature of energy is to form and dissolve continually. By not accepting this reality, by blocking the flow of energy, we invite suffering. Whenever we withdraw from phenomena or grasp them, there is irritation. Even when we achieve pleasure, it is surrounded by the hassle to realize it and the pain of losing it. Even if we are seemingly quite comfortable with life, there is some sense of uneasiness underneath the surface comfort. Moreover, not only is the seeming world out there continually changing and therefore painful, but there is something wrong with our home, our inner space. Our best friend, our ego, our constant companion who consoles and entertains us, is also not solid, also is born and dies continually.

The fact that ego does not exist as a solid entity, that we are fundamentally alone, is frightening. So we churn out thoughts, memories, and emotions to obscure the fact. As long as we are always busy, the fact of egolessness cannot be recognized. In fact, speeding is the strategy we employ to hide all three aspects of reality. Instead of seeing the changing nature of things we impulsively jump from thing to thing. Instead of acknowledging the underlying dissatisfaction in our lives we cover it up by highlighting, recalling and anticipating pleasures and comforts or slights and sorrows. Deception, evasion, ignoring is the way of ego.

In order to begin to see life as it is we need some method of cutting through the speed and deception in our lives. Sitting meditation provides a way of allowing the mind to slow down, to untangle itself. We neither feed nor repress thoughts but clearly see them without getting caught by them. Usually techniques that cut the chain of thoughts are used as aids—attention to the breath is most common. Calming the frenzied thought process is often quite painful since we allow thoughts and feelings that are normally repressed to emerge. So the turbulence may seem to increase before it subsides.

But along with the boredom, the irritation, the embarrassment, the inanity, the ups and downs of the meditation process, a heightened clarity begins to develop. There is more sense of being present, of a calm, precise relationship to things. Then this expands into an awareness of the environment in which phenomena occur. Meditation becomes a pervasive aspect of our everyday lives. We become more open, aware and permissive to whatever arises. We begin to see the realities of impermanence, suffering, and egolessness. These realities are not viewed as the unfortunate, harsh nature of things which must be overcome by reason and effort. Our efforts to build eternity on top of death, to create pleasure out of pain, to solidify ourselves in the face of aloneness—all these are futile. It is only by fully opening to death, pain and aloneness that their terrifying and tragic quality is overcome. And to overcome the terror they evoke is the gateway to sanity.

```
                f
               ull
              moon


  n      o     cl     o      u      d      s                                    s
                                                                            n   o
                                                                          s n o     w
                                                                 s   n         o       w
                                                                 s    n         o     w
                  b      u       t
                                              s

                  e        m        p                        n       o       m
                                                                   o
      t           y                                             n        w
                                                                    k
                              m      o      u      n      t      a      i      n
  s                 k           y
                                           m                      monastryyrtsanom
                                       o                        monastryyrtsanommonastry
                                                              monasrtyyrtsanommonastryyrtsa
                                              o              monastryyrtanommonastryyrtanom
                                                             monastrymonkmonkmonkmonktryyrt
                                                             monamonkmonkmoknmonkmonkmonom
                                                            monstrymmmmmmmmmmmmmmmmmmmmmmmm
              m                           u   m      m                   t      a
                        m                                 m      m            m      i      n
                                  n
                                              0000000000000000000
  00000000        0o0000000000                           00o00000
                                 00000000000000000      0000oo0ooooo0o000
                  t
      a
```

68

Karmê-Chöling and the Three Jewels

The Buddhist tradition is essentially non-theistic. It is not based on worship of an external entity but rather on an interaction of three principles, often called the "three jewels": buddha, dharma and sangha. The buddha principle is one of example—Buddha's example that human beings can work on themselves, discover basic truths and actually transcend confusion. This example is embodied in the lineage of gurus from Buddha down to the present time. Dharma is the path by which this process is accessible to any of us; it is the intellectual teaching and meditative practice, transmitted to us by the guru, which makes the journey possible. Sangha is the community of those on the path, the friends and enemies, lovers, colleagues, husbands and wives who are also dedicated to the dharma and who, at Karmê-Chöling, provide the daily environment of life.

These three principles must be considered aspects of a single principle. Complete practice requires the presence of all three and any imbalance can present problems and create obstacles. Underemphasis of the buddha aspect results in both insufficient inspiration and the danger of uncontrolled ego-growth. Relationship with a guru is necessary to provide a personal connection with the teachings as well as a periodic cutting through of one's habitual patterns and egocentric attitudes. Underemphasis of the dharma aspect can create a situation in which the path becomes a purely social phenomenon. Without a serious commitment to study of the teachings and practice of prescribed meditative techniques, one's involvement is essentially empty. Just associating with the guru is like taking a placebo when you are ill. It might make you feel better for a while, but without the real medicine of practice, your confusion is not helped. Underemphasis of the sangha aspect cuts off the strength that can be derived from communication with others on the path and can create a somewhat unreal practice. Compassion, an integral part of the path, cannot develop in isolation. There is no great value in meditation or study unless one can relate with others; and understanding, as opposed to intellectual accumulation, cannot develop without the living experience of human interchange.

If we accept the reality of these principles and the fact of their importance, then we must conclude that they offer us an excellent framework for evaluating our lives. Generally, we choose to forego this evaluation, perhaps because of a distrust of "judgment." But possibly this is also because of the comfort there is in just letting things go on without knowing quite what is going on. The notion that the three principles must all be present and be in balance can provide a very revealing basis for evaluation. It might be interesting here to have a look at Karmê-Chöling in terms of the three jewels.

Karmê-Chöling is a center established for the purpose of providing an environment for the study, practice and living of Buddhism. It is regarded as the major contemplative center of Vajradhatu, the association of Buddhist centers founded by and under the guidance of Chögyam Trungpa, Rinpoche. In the five years since its founding, Karmê-Chöling has experienced serious problems and undergone fundamental changes which can be understood in terms of the balance of buddha, dharma and sangha principles. In the beginning the deficiency probably involved all three areas. The inspirational aspect of the guru (the buddha principle) was very strongly present, but an equally vital function of the guru is interference with ego-building. Not surprisingly, in the case of Karmê-Chöling there was a great initial resistance to the ego-cutting role of the guru. Most Americans of this generation have grown up in an atmosphere of rejecting discipline and of challenging any sort of authority. With this kind of background, most students found it extraordinarily difficult to relate to such concepts as "truth," "wisdom," "discipline," and so on, which they were in the habit of considering empty rhetoric.

The indulgent styles of most students, coupled with the extreme busyness of establishing a center also limited the unfolding of the dharma principle. Meditation practice was optional and sporadic and study was an individual matter if and when it was engaged in. And as far as the sangha principle is concerned, of course a community was beginning to form at this point but it is dubious if it could have been called "sangha" just yet. Rinpoche has described the dynamic of sangha as " . . . one person gives up the idea of his ego territory and begins to work with life situations as they are; and because of this another person is inspired." However in the early days of Karmê-Chöling this was not quite the case. There was a great deal of ego-colliding and fighting for territory which certainly didn't seem like giving up anything. In retrospect, however, it can be seen as the beginning stages of coming to terms with the problem of ego.

In his book, *Meditation in Action,* Rinpoche talks about the "manure of experience." He states that the wise practitioner does not try to throw away all of his negative, unpleasant, smelly qualities but rather utilizes them as a farmer does manure. The idea is to acknowledge, study and make friends with these qualities. Then they become the working basis, the material for one's practice. But there is also a warning given—utilizing does not mean collecting further manure endlessly. The right time arrives to stop collecting these riches. In its early period Karmê-Chöling was still collecting and not yet using. But it was not long before steps were taken to bring the three-jewels principle into greater play and greater balance. Gradually but effectively the sorting-out process that led to the selection of community members and the development of personal relationships with Rinpoche brought the buddha principle into greater prominence. But certainly the most important development was Rinpoche's gradually and methodically increased emphasis on the practice of meditation.

The Buddhist teachings present meditation as the only way to work with the tight and incredibly tenacious grip of ego. Meditation practice allows an opportunity for gaps to be perceived in the midst of our usual mental churning. This, in turn, opens up a subtle sense of spaciousness and lends a certain transparency to the concerns of self-protection and self-expansion that we fixate on so compulsively. Since both the buddha and sangha principles depend so greatly on surrendering self-involvement and opening to a larger situation, meditation practice, which belongs to the dharma principle, is essential to both of them.

Looking at the present situation at Karmê-Chöling, meditation practice has increased to the point where it thoroughly pervades the life of the center. The daily schedule now includes four-and-a-half hours of group meditation. There are also two hours of formal study. In addition to this the community does bi-weekly nyinthuns (daylong meditation sessions), and dathuns (monthlong meditation sessions) twice each year. It is impossible to overstate the effect this increase in meditation practice has had on the community.

Also we observe that both the inspirational and ego-corrective effects of the guru are now far more apparent. Just as on a personal level the proper practice of mindfulness allows the senses to perceive new subtleties, so also the proper involvement in practice allows the community and the teacher to relate to increasingly subtle problems together.

The intensified practice and study have become an integral and ordinary part of the residents' lives and brought a quality of maturity to daily work and interaction with each other. The traditional triple role of the sangha—working on ourselves, spreading the dharma, and following a qualified teacher—has become a reality.

Interestingly this state of affairs at Karmê-Chöling does not seem to depend on individuals. The population of the center is quite changeable apart from a basic staff; and even the composition of the staff is constantly changing, though more slowly. But the strength of the three jewels in balance appears to thrive regardless of changes in personnel. In addition, as new community members and visitors come to Karmê-Chöling they do not have to go through the same lengthy evolution as the early members did. Newcomers seem to absorb quickly what came to the early students in long, painful stages. Although it is, of course, still necessary to work with developing balance on the individual level, the evolution of the situation itself seems to absorb individuals into its style, rather than the other way around.

Staff members of Karmê-Chöling now conduct introductory workshops as well as long practice and study sessions. The great success and value of these programs is clearly related to the long and manual process that the center has undergone since founding. Something very powerful has happened at Karmê-Chöling. Undoubtedly the strong presence and gradually achieved balance of the three jewels, is both the cause and the result.

Seal of office of the Trungpa tulkus.

Cynical Letter

Licking honey from a razor blade,
Eyes of the learned gouged out by books,
The beauty of maidens worn by display,
The warrior dead from lack of fear—
It is ironical to see the dharma of samsara,
Celebrities deafened by fame,
The hand of the artist crippled by rheumatism.

The moth flew into the oil lamp,
The blind man walks with a torch,
The cripple runs in his wheelchair,
A fool's rhetoric is deep and learned,
The poet laughs himself to death.
The religious spin circles in accordance with religion,
If they had not practiced their religion, they could not spin;
The sinner cannot spin according to religion,
He spins according to not knowing how to spin.
The yogis spin by practicing yoga,
If they don't have chakras to spin, they are not yogis.
Chögyam is spinning, watching the spinning/samsara;
If there is no samsara/spinning, there is no Chögyam.

May 22, 1972

His Holiness the 16th Gyalwa Karmapa giving blessings during his recent trip.

The Visit of His Holiness
the Gyalwa Karmapa to the United States

In 1974 His Holiness Rangjung Rigpe Dorje, the sixteenth Gyalwa Karmapa, supreme head of the Kagyu lineage, came to America as the guest of Chögyam Trungpa, Rinpoche, and the Vajradhatu communities. He came with a large company of monks, translators and attendants, and was received according to the lavish traditions of the lineage. These traditions were largely comprised of forms which had to be observed fully and very precisely. But the forms seemed to have a very rich meaning and, as the tour of America unfolded, we discovered in them a sense of spontaneity and recognition, in that they naturally expressed what we felt in relation to His Holiness.

Preparations for the visit actually began ten months before His Holiness' arrival when Sister Palmo Khechog, a Buddhist nun and one of His Holiness' personal translators, visited the Vajradhatu centers as Rinpoche's guest and His Holiness' emissary. There followed for us the most intensive period of work and training we had ever experienced as Rinpoche's students. In Vermont, New York, Colorado, and California, building was undertaken and facilities refurbished to provide a suitably elegant and majestic environment for the reception of the sixteenth Gyalwa Karmapa. Teams of craftsmen, following designs drawn up by Rinpoche, produced a multitude of artifacts and special furnishings to complement the living quarters of the Tibetan traveling party as well as the various shrine rooms and meeting halls where ceremonies and audiences would take place. Carpenters, wood-carvers and seamstresses collaborated to produce three huge thrones and several smaller ones. The three big ones were elaborately decorated with colorfully painted wood carvings, hung with embroidered silks and seated with huge gold brocade cushions. These were used for the rites at Karma Dzong (the Vajradhatu center in Boulder, Colorado) and for the Vajra Crown ceremony, which His Holiness performed in New York, Colorado and California. The smaller ones were used for formal audiences and various rites and empowerments.

His Holiness arrived in New York on September 11th. He was greeted at the airplane in traditional fashion by Rinpoche and the members of the New York Dharmadhatu. (The Dharmadhatus are the centers for Rinpoche's students in the various North American cities.) As prescribed by custom Rinpoche appeared holding offerings of incense; there was the presentation of white scarves, flowers and, later at the Dharmadhatu, the formal offering of rice and buttered tea. Intense tutoring in protocol had been given to Rinpoche's students to prepare them for this moment and Michael Chender, as coordinator of the New York Dharmadhatu, bravely stepped forward to be the first American greeting Karmapa on this continent. Apparently His Holiness had been doing his own study of Western customs for he returned the greeting with an American handshake. News of the handshake was immediately phoned to Vermont, Colorado and California, along with the incredible message that His Holiness was actually a tremendously warm, friendly, and delightful person to relate to. The sense of warmth, joy, and genuine relationship became a keynote of the visit.

At that point His Holiness' party consisted of nine Tibetan monks, Sister Palmo and two translators. From the airport His Holiness and retinue were cavalcaded to the secluded estate of Mr. C. T. Shen, one of the foremost patrons of Buddhism in America, where they lived during their stay in New York. There the members of the Dharmadhatu were introduced to His Holiness by Rinpoche. They presented gifts and salutations and received His Holiness' blessings. For the next few days His Holiness was hosted about New York by Rinpoche and the Dharmadhatu. There was a reception for them at a large hotel and meetings with various municipal officials and other dignitaries. The culmination of that visit occurred on September 21 when His Holiness performed the Vajra Crown ceremony before a large audience. The Vajra Crown ceremony is a rite which only His Holiness

can perform that confers the power of his lineage. Afterwards, the entire audience filed on stage one by one to bow and receive his blessings. His Holiness then joined his monks at the Dharmadhatu shrine hall where they were preparing for the Karma Pakshi abhiseka, given later that evening.

After the abhiseka or empowerment, Rinpoche went ahead to Tail of the Tiger, the Vajradhatu center in Vermont, to supervise the last hours of arrangements for His Holiness' visit there. This established a basic pattern for the rest of the trip. Rinpoche would fly ahead a few days early to oversee the finishing touches at each center. When the traveling party finally arrived, they would be greeted by the sound of Tibetan horns and, surrounded by his students, Rinpoche would step forward with sticks of incense to welcome His Holiness once again. Any place where His Holiness was received would be richly decorated with huge silk banners, thangkas, Chinese and Japanese brocade and strangely designed furniture which must have been familiar to the Tibetans. His Holiness' meals were served on special trays and tables designed by Rinpoche and executed by Vajradhatu craftsmen. Literally hundreds of artifacts were specially prepared for His Holiness' use in America. This produced a minor revolution in their approach to design among the Vajradhatu artisans. They were introduced to all sorts of new ideas in jewelry, painting, woodworking and cloth design by that famous Tibetan interior decorator, Trungpa Rinpoche.

From New York the company was driven to Tail of the Tiger. Driving through Vermont and New Hampshire gave His Holiness his first good look at American countryside, which he found very impressive and, as he constantly remarked, rather neatly arranged. By this time other individuals had been added to the traveling party, which became an extremely impressive phenomenon with monks, bodyguards, chauffeurs, attendants and translators. A simple stop for lunch would be an affair planned a week in advance. One such prearranged stop was an inn in New Hampshire where rooms had been specially decorated and prepared for lunch and the hotel staff briefed on how to serve a Tibetan dignitary. Strangely enough, they did this with perfectly appropriate feeling. His Holiness seemed to carry with him his own special atmosphere of dignity, care, and lightheartedness, which infected everyone.

The party arrived at Tail of the Tiger that evening. The road up to the main house was lined with friends of the community and students of Rinpoche's who had gathered from all around New England. Monks playing oboelike Tibetan horns stood before the entrance as Rinpoche met His Holiness once again and brought him to a living room decked out with brocades and finery and outfitted with a throne. Once again bowls of rice and Tibetan tea were served. Then the hundred or so people who had come for the reception entered to be introduced by Rinpoche, bow, present gifts and receive blessings. Later that evening the whole party, swelled by the addition of an American and a French translator, were conducted to Rinpoche's house on the other side of the property. This would be His Holiness' home in Vermont. Rinpoche saw His Holiness and party off as they left the main house. They arrived a few minutes later at Rinpoche's house to find Rinpoche again waiting at the front door flanked by the ubiquitous attendants. His Holiness later remarked that the American students of the dharma must have wings, because everywhere he looked from New York to California he saw the same people standing there politely in attendance and ready to serve.

That evening the Tail of the Tiger community was privately presented to His Holiness and he spoke to them briefly. They chanted the supplication to the Kagyu lineage and the "four dharmas of Gampopa." This fascinated the Tibetan monks who had never heard those chants in any language other than Tibetan. They seemed rather moved by them and one monk hastened to tell us through a translator that we had "chanted very sweetly." They in turn chanted the supplication to the lineage for us in Tibetan. We came to be very good friends with the monks. There was a strong sense of mutual recognition as if we somehow belonged to the same family. Among them were several young incarnate lamas, Tenga Rinpoche (the master of ceremonies at Rumtek, the seat of the Gyalwa Karmapas in Sikkim) and one venerable monk who led the chanting in a remarkable deep voice.

The next day His Holiness and Rinpoche hosted a gathering of the local clergy who spent an afternoon drinking tea and asking questions about the Buddhist religion and its future in the West. Rinpoche was translator for His Holiness at that meeting and relations were very warm and lighthearted. The tea ended with one of the guests asking His Holiness if he could do anything at that moment to help the various religions in working with youth in America. This had been a principle topic of conversation. He answered by chanting once more the supplication to the Kagyu lineage. One by one the monks and translators gathered from all over the house to join in the chanting, and the meeting ended on that impressive note.

His Holiness rested at Tail of the Tiger several days. During that time he spoke personally with many of the community members, asked and answered many questions, and day by day blessed different portions of the property. It was a time of great joy for all of us, not only because of the pleasure of serving His Holiness, but also because of the intense sense of community which developed as we worked at a peak of efficiency to make his stay a perfect one. Rinpoche gently guided us to the momentous realization that we did not really need three hours of sleep a night as much as we thought. Then he proved to us that three hours of sleep a night was a tremendous luxury.

The day after his arrival His Holiness gave the Karma Pakshi empowerment to the community. We had stayed up until five o'clock that morning receiving instructions from Rinpoche concerning the abhiseka. Rinpoche translated significant portions of the text into English and extensive notes were taken. By the time the party reached Snowmass, Colorado, the site of the Vajradhatu seminary, the notes from Rinpoche's preparatory training sessions had become a work in themselves. Teachers at the seminary edited them into a short book, which included a description of the abhiseka and Rinpoche's translations of the ceremony and parts of the Karma Pakshi sadhana.

His Holiness' last day at Tail of the Tiger was spent mainly in blessing the retreat huts, selecting locations for new retreat facilities and in performing the long Mahakala sadhana for the benefit of the entire center. Looking over the property he remarked, "This is indeed the land of Milarepa." That evening he met with the executive committee of Tail of the Tiger at his house. Rinpoche had already left for Colorado, but not before requesting that His Holiness give the center a Tibetan name. The name he chose was Karmê Chö-kyi-ling, which means "Dharma Place of the Karma Kagyus." He suggested we use the shortened form of this, Karmê-Chöling. His Holiness then gave a talk to the executive committee on Karmê-Chöling's role and future. He said that he was very pleased and inspired by the Dharmadhatu and Karmê-Chöling. He said that if we continued as we had been proceeding, "The dharma will spread in America like wildfire on a mountain." He then spoke about what would be skillful means in relation to social and political situations in America and gave very penetrating advice. He left with us a large art book that had been given to him, remarking that since he had left it behind he would have to return soon. He also presented the community with a Mahakala thangka and various artifacts which now stand on the shrine, including a statue of the Buddha.

The next day the enlarged caravan continued on the next leg of its journey. Leaving Karmê-Chöling, His Holiness admired the farms in the area and said, "This place is so beautiful, I'm going to build a big stupa here one day." On the way to Boston he again showed great interest in the countryside and made comparisons with Tibetan land. He asked many questions about American agriculture. It developed that one of his principle impressions of America was of an extremely organized society. He admired whatever efficiency and sense of discipline he saw in the environment and people around him. Rinpoche's own demands on his students in terms of discipline, organization and endurance were greater than ever yet during the American tour. After the Vajra Crown rite in Boulder, His Holiness again praised us for our efficiency and application, comparing us to his own monks. That was actually a very generous comparison, for the monks not only did their duties well, but with a characteristic sense of effortlessness and simplicity.

We drove to Logan International Airport where the group was received by the Boston Dharmadhatu. There was a public reception at the airport followed by a meeting with the Dharmadhatu members who prostrated and presented gifts, following the pattern set in New York and Vermont.

From there His Holiness flew to Ann Arbor, Michigan, where he was the guest of Swami Muktananda, who was also touring America at that time. They appeared together for a convocation and gave talks on Hindu and Buddhist dharma. His Holiness spoke briefly on the three yanas. Swami Muktananda spoke at greater length on devotion to the guru. They discussed together communication across language barriers, using three-way translation from Tibetan to English to Marati and back. The next day the Swami gave an outdoor luncheon for His Holiness and a large gathering of disciples. The members of the Ann Arbor Dharmadhatu presented themselves as before and then had a very long and remarkable private interview with His Holiness at which was discussed many aspects of their practice and work as students of Rinpoche. Then a member of the Dharmadhatu who spoke Tibetan drove His Holiness and company on a sightseeing tour of the area and then to the airport, where they boarded a plane for Boulder.

Karma Dzong, the Vajradhatu capital, was the highlight of the American tour. Everything that had happened before happened there on a much larger scale. His Holiness performed the Vajra Crown rite again for a very large audience. He gave a series of lineage abhisekas to the Karma Dzong community and the Mahakala empowerment to a smaller group of students. There were meetings with officers of Vajradhatu and discussions held with different groups of students. His Holiness attended various receptions at the centers and blessed the community houses and Nalanda facilities in Boulder.

The intense energy of that week reached a zenith on the evening of the lineage abhisekas. At the close of the last ceremony Tenga Rinpoche stood up and read to the community a formidable Tibetan document composed by His Holiness, followed by an English translation.

In it he proclaimed Rinpoche a holder of the Kagyu lineage and an accomplished vajra master. (*See below,* pp. 86-87.) The party left Boulder after a week to visit the Rocky Mountain Dharma Center in northern Colorado, another Vajradhatu meditation center.

The next stop on the tour was the Vajradhatu Seminary in Snowmass, Colorado. As we escorted His Holiness to the main building of the seminary, he gaily pointed to a fire burning on a ski slope and said, "You see, 'like wildfire on a mountain.'" At the seminary the same processes as in Boulder occurred on a smaller scale. Seminarians witnessed the Vajra Crown rite and received the Karma Pakshi abhiseka, as well as the most thorough preparation for the rites yet. There were private meetings with the staff of the seminary and groups of Rinpoche's students working on specific projects. In keeping with the Boulder Proclamation, His Holiness asked that Rinpoche participate with him in the giving of abhiseka at the Snowmass ceremonies.

Leaving the Vajradhatu Seminary, His Holiness and party were driven to Dorje Khyung Dzong, the Vajradhatu retreat center in Southern Colorado, which His Holiness found especially pleasing and which he inspected carefully and blessed. Moving further southwest, we visited the Great Kiva at the American Indian archaeological site at Aztec, New Mexico. The Kiva was impressive and His Holiness indicated similarities between the ancient Indian ritual objects and architecture and those of Tibet. We continued on to Canyon de Chelly in the Navajo lands, another place of former importance in Indian life. Some of the monks seemed especially drawn to the place, joking about previous incarnations there and teasing one another about how soft their present lives were. His Holiness was quite interested, but seemed mainly to want to know about *living* Indians. Were they like the tribes of wild savages in Eastern Tibet? Were they fantastically, fabulously wealthy? Our arrival in the mesa land of the Hopi undeceived him; everywhere we went was an air of poverty and of desperation, because the entire summer had been without rain. When visiting the kiva at Polacca, His Holiness stopped to chant beside the entrance. Later that day, seemingly miraculously, it rained. In the evening His Holiness decided suddenly to perform an empowerment rite (that of Avalokitesvara) for the Hopi. The Hopi came in their pick-up trucks through the fresh mud bringing offerings of fried bread and *piki* and the occasion was a very moving one. The next day's edition of *Eagle's Cry* ran the headline: "Tibetan Chief Brings Rain." It was with a feeling of great celebration that the party traveled on to the Grand Canyon. From there His Holiness and party drove to Phoenix where they enplaned for San Francisco.

San Francisco was the last stage on the tour of the United States. His Holiness' party arrived in the middle of the ten-day Dharma Festival of the Arts held by the California Dharmadhatus and Padma Jong, another Vajradhatu retreat center. There followed the same pattern of blessings, sightseeing and audiences with Rinpoche's students. His Holiness also met with various Buddhist teachers on the West Coast such as Tarthang Tulku and

Richard Baker, Roshi, successor to Suzuki Roshi as head of Tassajara and the California Zen Center communities. Mrs. Shunryu Suzuki, widow of Suzuki Roshi, served His Holiness tea formally in the Japanese manner, in what was an extremely dignified and touching encounter. Before leaving San Francisco, His Holiness performed the Vajra Crown ceremony once more before 2,500 people.

On October 18, His Holiness left our care to begin a tour of Canadian Buddhist Centers and then to continue on to Europe.

*His Holiness
performing the
Vajra Crown rite.*

DHARMA CHAKRA CENTER
RUMTEK, GANGTOK
SIKKIM.

Proclamation to All Those Who Dwell Under the Sun Upholding the Tradition of the Spiritual & Temporal Orders

The ancient & renowned lineage of the Trungpas, since the great siddha Trungmase Chö-kyi Gyamtso Lodrö, possessor of only holy activity, has in every generation given rise to great beings. Awakened by the vision of these predecessors in the lineage, this my present lineage holder, Chö-kyi Gyamtso Trungpa Rinpoche, supreme incarnate being, has magnificently carried out the vajra-holder's discipline in the land of America, bringing about the liberation of students & ripening them in the dharma. This wonderful truth is clearly manifest.

Accordingly, I empower Chögyam Trungpa *Vajra Holder & Possessor of The Victory Banner of The Practice Lineage of The Karma Kagyu.* Let this be recognized by all people of both elevated & ordinary station.

This proclamation is written at the glorious dharma center of Karma Dzong by the sixteenth Karmapa in the year of the wooden tiger, the eighth month, the thirteenth day; September 29, 1974.

Yantra of Vasudhara, which brings wealth.